Casting
for
Crafters

Casting
for
Crafters

Marie Browning

Sterling Publishing Co., Inc.
New York

Prolific Impressions Production Staff:
Editor in Chief: Mickey Baskett
Copy Editor: Phyllis Mueller
Graphics: KRT Graphics
Styling: Lenos Key
Photography: Jerry Mucklow Rocket Photography, Vision West Photography
Administration: Jim Baskett

Library of Congress Cataloging-in-Publication Data

Browning, Marie.
  Casting for crafters / Marie Browning.
      p. cm.
  Includes index.
  ISBN-13: 978-1-4027-2446-6
  ISBN-10: 1-4027-2446-2
  1. Modeling. I. Title.
  TT916.B76 2006
  745.5--dc22

2005032773

10 9 8 7 6 5 4 3 2 1

Published by Sterling Publishing Co., Inc.
387 Park Avenue South, New York, N.Y. 10016

©2006 by Prolific Impressions, Inc.
Produced by Prolific Impressions, Inc.
160 South Candler St., Decatur, GA 30030
Distributed in Canada by Sterling Publishing
c/o Canadian Manda Group, 165 Dufferin Street
Toronto, Ontario, Canada M6K 3H6
Distributed in the United Kingdom by GMC Distribution Services,
Castle Place, 166 High Street, Lewes, East Sussex, England BN7 1XU
Distributed in Australia by Capricorn Link (Australia) Pty. Ltd.
P.O. Box 704, Windsor, NSW 2756 Australia

Sterling ISBN-13: 978-1-4027-2446-6
          iSBN-10: 1-4027-2446-2

For information about custom editions, special sales, premium and corporate purchases, please contact Sterling Special Sales Department at 800-805-5489 or specialsales@sterlingpub.com.

ACKNOWLEDGMENTS

I thank these manufacturers for their generous contributions of quality products and support in the creation of the projects in this book.

For casting plaster, mold making products, wire mesh:
Activa Products Inc., Marshall, TX, USA, www.activaproducts.com

For two-part epoxy resin, EasyCast, polyester casting resin, rubber latex mold builder, measuring cups, disposable brushes, stir sticks, resin molds for knobs, jewelry, and paperweights:
Environmental Technology Inc., Fields Landing, CA, USA, www.eti-usa.com

For Poetry Stone kits, cement lettering systems, casting pigments, molds:
Magnetic Poetry, Minneapolis, MN, USA, www.magneticpoetry.com

For plastic cement, plaster, and soap molds:
Milky Way Molds, Portland, OR, USA, www.milkywaymolds.com

For Moldmaker polymer clay, Sculpey and Premo polymer clays, polymer clay tools, and polymer clay push molds:
Polyform Products, Elk Grove Village, IL, USA, www.sculpey.com

For plaster, mold making kits, and life casting kits:
Webster Group, Redlands, CA, USA, www.webstergroup.us

For molding plasters, casting pigments, plaster paint, pearl buffing powder, plaster sealer, plaster tools, and plaster, soap, and resin molds:
Yaley Enterprises Inc., Redding, CA, USA, www.yaley.com

About Marie Browning

Marie Browning is a consummate craft designer who has made a career of designing products, writing books and articles, and teaching and demonstrating. You may have been charmed by her creative acumen but not been aware of the woman behind it; she has designed stencils, stamps, transfers, and a variety of other award-winning product lines for art and craft supply companies. As well as writing numerous books on creative living, Marie's articles and designs have appeared in numerous home decor and crafts magazines. Marie Browning earned a Fine Arts Diploma from Camosun College and attended the University of Victoria. She is a Certified Professional Demonstrator, a design member of the Crafts and Hobby Association (CHA), and a board member of the Society of Craft Designers (SCD). Marie also serves on the committee for SCD that researches and writes about upcoming trends in the arts and crafts industry. In 2004 she was selected by *Craftrends* trade publication as a Top Influential Industry Designer.

She lives, gardens, and crafts on Vancouver Island in Canada. She and her husband Scott have three children: Katelyn, Lena, and Jonathan. Marie can be contacted at www.mariebrowning.com

OTHER BOOKS BY MARIE BROWNING PUBLISHED BY STERLING

Paper Mosaics (2006)

Snazzy Jars (2006)

Jazzy Baskets (2005)

Purse Pizzazz (2005)

Really Jazzy Jars (2005)

Totally Cool Polymer Clay for Kids (2005)

Totally Cool Soapmaking for Kids (2004, reprinted in softcover)

Wonderful Wraps (2003, reprinted in softcover)

Jazzy Jars (2003, reprinted in softcover)

Designer Soapmaking (2003, reprinted in German)

300 Recipes for Soap (2002, reprinted in softcover and in French)

Crafting with Vellum and Parchment (2001, reprinted in softcover with the title *New Paper Crafts*)

Melt & Pour Soapmaking (2000, reprinted in softcover)

Hand Decorating Paper (2000, reprinted in softcover)

Memory Gifts (2000, reprinted in softcover with the title *Family Photocrafts*)

Making Glorious Gifts from Your Garden (1999, reprinted in softcover)

Handcrafted Journals, Albums, Scrapbooks & More (1999, (reprinted in softcover)

Beautiful Handmade Natural Soaps (1998, reprinted in softcover with the title *Natural Soapmaking*)

contents

CONTENTS

cast, casting, v. (kăst) 1. To form (liquid metal, for example) into a particular shape by pouring into a mold.

Ice cubes, gelatin, homemade chocolates, and cement patios are everyday examples of casting, the act or process of making casts or molds. The procedure of pouring a material into a mold, letting it cure, then unmolding it is a very simple process you can use to create projects for your home and garden, to hold memories, and to make gifts.

Casting materials are also familiar to us. Doctors wrap our limbs with plaster when we break our bones, we walk on cast concrete sidewalks, and we use cured resins (plastics) every day that were formed in molds.

This book explores different types of craft casting using clear resins, plaster, cement, and hypertufa. For the projects, I selected user-friendly materials that were easy to find and produced the best results.

Beginning casters can have the benefit of my successes and my failures – I have included step-by-step instructions and numerous tips to ensure your success the very first time. Projects include cast resin jewelry pieces with the look of glass and semi-precious stones, frames, and art objects. I also developed some new resin casting techniques, such as Collection Casting and Cast Mat Frames. You can use these techniques to create a variety of stylish and practical home decor items such as coasters, cabinet knobs, switchplates, tiles, bowls, and soap dishes.

Cast plaster pieces can be used to embellish frames and furniture and add decorative touches to home decor. Casting with cement is a great family activity – you'll find projects for creating concrete and hypertufa garden accents that you will enjoy for a long time.

I hope you enjoy your casting experiences.

Marie Browning

a brief history of casting

Casting technology can be traced back almost 5,500 years BCE in Mesopotamia when people used clay molds to cast copper into bowls. Gold and silver were also used for casting, but copper was the material of choice to create early tools. The basic process involved a liquid casting material poured into a mold created in sand. The oldest casting in existence today is a cast copper frog made in a simple sand mold.

The Chinese developed iron casting around 1,000 BCE, and steel was created in India in 500 BCE. Many early metal castings were poured in sand molds.

The oldest indication of plaster casting is almost 9,000 years old. The ancient Egyptians burned gypsum in open-air fires, pounded it into powder, and mixed it with water to make jointing materials for their temples. They also used plaster to make life-cast masks. Concrete and cement have also been used for many centuries. Gypsum, an ingredient in plaster, is also the base material for concrete.

Natural polymers, in the form of horns, waxes, and gums from tropical trees, have been used to cast objects for centuries. At the beginning of the 19th century, scientific advances in the fields of chemistry and physics produced materials with properties that were not found in nature. Cellulose nitrate (celluloid), the first successful plastic, was developed in 1862 while looking for a substitute for the ivory billiard ball. Casein, a turn of the century plastic made with fat-free milk and resins, was used to make buttons, fountain pens, and knitting needles.

In the early 20th century, carbolic acid and formaldehyde were mixed to form Bakelite, the first synthetic plastic, which was used to make cast household items like clocks, radios, telephones, and car components and jewelry. Colorless urea resin, polyvinyl chloride plastics, and clear acrylics followed in the 1930s.

From 1935 to 1945, the war effort resulted in the development of synthetic plastics, including silicones, epoxy, and polyester resins. In the 1960s, the modern crafting industry began with the popularity of resin crafted clear cast grapes. (You can still find them in high-end gift stores.) While researching and creating projects for this book, I found the amount of casting materials and mold-making materials available to home crafters overwhelming – they can be found in crafts, art supply, and hardware stores and home improvement centers.

Molds & mold-making techniques

No matter what type of material you wish to cast, you will need a mold. This chapter explores the types of molds you can use for any casting material. Techniques are presented for creating a mold master, making a mold from polymer clay, making a sand cast mold, making a rubber mold, and supporting molds.

Choosing a Mold

The choice of the casting material is the first decision you make when beginning a casting project, but since most casting techniques require a mold, the second decision is the mold you will use.

The following chart provides a quick reference for most common molds and the casting materials you can use with them. Each has advantages and disadvantages. Please be aware that because of the huge variety of molds and casting materials, *this is general information only.* There are variations and exceptions.

PLASTIC MOLDS FOR CANDY, PLASTER, CONCRETE & SOAP

Use: Casting plaster, polymer clay, concrete; also candy, soap, wax

Advantages
+ Can be used for multiple castings
+ Many designs available, good to excellent detail
+ Mostly inexpensive

Disadvantages
- Some molds unsuitable for high temperature castings
- Must be tested before using with resins – most do not work
- Cannot be used for food after craft casting
- Some need to be supported to level
- Cannot create your own
- Need mold release
- Some large concrete molds very expensive

PLASTIC POLYPROPYLENE MOLDS

Use: Excellent for crystal clear resin casting; also soap, wax

Advantages
+ Available in knob, jewelry, small object designs
+ Can be used for multiple castings
+ Excellent detail

Disadvantages
- Limited designs available
- Mold release needed (except for polyester resin casting)
- More expensive
- Cannot create your own

MOLDS MADE OF POLYMER CLAY

Use: Casting plaster, polymer clay; cannot be used with resins

Advantages
+ Easy to create yourself
+ Can be used for multiple castings
+ Can be re-formed repeatedly before curing
+ Can be baked in home oven to cure
+ Creates molds with reasonably good details

Disadvantages
- Best with smaller castings
- Can not be used with resins
- More expensive to create
- Easy to distort while casting polymer clay

RUBBER MOLDS OF NATURAL LATEX

Use: Casting plaster, concrete, resins; also soap, wax

Advantages
+ Easy to create yourself
+ Excellent detail
+ Inexpensive way to produce your own molds

Disadvantages
- Longer process for creating mold
- Needs backup mold or support
- Needs mold release

RUBBER MOLDS OF SYNTHETIC LATEX

Use: Casting plaster, resins; also soap, wax

Advantages
+ Easy to create yourself
+ Excellent detail
+ Inexpensive to produce

Disadvantages
- More expensive than natural latex
- Mold coloring can come off on casting
- Longer process for creating mold
- Needs backup mold or support
- Needs mold release

continued on page 14

Types of Molds

Pictured: 1. Sand; 2. Polypropylene; 3. Soap; 4. Plastic candy; 5. Concrete; 6. Jewelry mold for resin casting; 7. Plaster;
8. Rubber (natural latex); 9. Polymer clay mold; 10. Rubber (synthetic latex)

Choosing a Mold, continued

SILICONE RUBBER MOLDS

Use: Casting plaster, concrete, polymer clay, casting resins, soap, wax, foods

Advantages	**Disadvantages**
+ Excellent detail	- Complex to mix and create yourself
+ Excellent designs available in pre-made molds	- Expensive, whether you buy them or make them yourself
+ Can be used for multiple castings	- Needs mold release for casting resins
+ Can create yourself	- Produces matte finish for resin castings

SAND MOLD

Use: Casting plaster, concrete, wax, hypertufa

Advantages	**Disadvantages**
+ Very inexpensive	- Can be used only once
+ Easy to create your own mold	- Very little detail, even with fine sand
+ No mold release needed	
+/- Sand becomes part of casting	

Mold Requirements

When choosing a mold, it's important to consider how flexible the mold material is, how rigid the cured casting will be, and whether or not the mold has undercuts. (Undercuts are the small spaces in the mold that hold the casting material. In some materials, undercuts can make it impossible to release the casting after it has cured.) Here are some examples:

- Flexible plastic molds can be used with rigid casting materials such as resins and plaster, but the casting cannot be created with undercuts.
- It is easy to pull a latex rubber mold away from a hard casting made with resin, but a large or detailed undercut could cause a softer plaster casting to break.
- Latex rubber, silicone rubber, and sand molds can have undercuts – they can be easily stretched or removed from the casting.
- When making your own rubber latex, silicone rubber, or polymer clay molds, carefully consider the casting materials you will use in the mold and if undercuts will be a problem.
- Never use molds for food after they have been used for casting non-edible materials. TIP: Since most plastic candy, chocolate, and ice molds are inexpensive, buy two, one for each use. Label them clearly "food" or "non-food."

In Doubt? Test!

To decide if a plastic candy mold can be used to cast resin, test it first. Generally, chocolate molds cannot be used as they cannot take the heat generated by the resin as it cures, and they will warp or leak. The casting will also be impossible to remove. Candy molds that are designed for hard candies may be used with resins, but should be tested first with a silicone, lecithin, or PVA mold release. CAUTION: **Never** use molds for food products after using as them for casting.

Testing your purchased molds with a casting material is easy. Turn the mold over. In one area apply a mold release. Apply a small amount of the casting material on the back in two areas, the area with the mold release and another untreated area. When the material has cured, see if it comes off easily or is hard to remove from the mold. This is an easy way to see if the casting material will be easy to release from the mold and if a mold release is necessary.

Mold Release Agents

The type of mold release you need depends on the material you are casting and the type of mold you are using. My best advice is to use the mold release the mold manufacturer recommends.

That said, here are some basic guidelines about mold release agents:

Powder: Polymer clay usually needs a light dusting of powder, such as body dusting powder or cornstarch, so it does not stick to molds. NOTE: When using polymer clay, you are making an impression with the mold. **Never** bake the clay in the mold.

PVA (polyvinyl alcohol) mold release provides an impervious barrier between the mold and the casting. It can be sprayed or wiped into molds; make sure any excess is wiped away. It sometimes is colored, and may leave a slight coloring to the casting. It also may leave a cloudy film on a resin casting.

Silicone-based mold release is sprayed or wiped into molds and the excess is wiped away. Many new silicone releases are nontoxic sprays that leave little residue on the casting.

Lecithin, derived from vegetable oil (usually soybean), makes a superb non-toxic mold release. Choose a paintable lecithin mold release if you wish to paint the casting after it is released from the mold.

Wax-based mold release can be as simple as carnauba car polish or furniture polish. They are wiped into molds and the excess is wiped away. Colored wax can slightly color the casting and may leave a film on polyester and epoxy resin castings. **Don't** use a wax mold release if you're planning to paint your casting.

Surfactant spray, while not technically a mold release, is sprayed into molds before pouring plaster and cement to reduce the bubbles on the surface of the cast piece. It is amazing the difference it makes for successful projects. Window cleaner or ammonia can also be used. Use the spray that the mold manufacturer recommends for best results.

Choosing Mold Releases

Mold	Casting Material	Recommended Mold Release
Plastic Candy Mold	Plaster	No mold release required; surfactant spray recommended.
	Epoxy resin	Not a recommended casting material for this mold, although there are a few exceptions. Test before casting.
	Polymer clay	Dust with powder or cornstarch; water can also be used. For making impressions only.
Plastic Mold for Concrete	Plaster	Use a light oil (vegetable or mineral oil) as a mold release.
	Concrete	Light oil (vegetable or mineral oil) or petroleum jelly.
Plastic Mold for Soap	Plaster	No mold release required.
	Epoxy resin	Not a recommended casting material for this mold, although there are a few exceptions. Test before casting.
	Concrete	Use a light oil (vegetable or mineral oil) or petroleum jelly as a mold release.
Polypropylene Mold	Polyester resin	No mold release required.
	Epoxy resin	Use the manufacturer's recommended mold release or a PVA, silicone, or lecithin-based release
Molds made from Polymer Clay	Plaster	No mold release required.
	Polymer clay	Dust with powder or cornstarch; water can also be used. For making impressions only.
Rubber Molds (Synthetic & Natural)	Plaster	No mold release required.
	Polyester resin	Use the mold manufacturer's recommended mold release or a PVA, silicon, or lecithin-based release.
	Epoxy resin	Use the mold manufacturer's recommended mold release or a PVA, silicon, or lecithin-based release.
	Concrete	Use the mold manufacturer's recommended mold release or a PVA, silicon, or lecithin-based release.
Sand Mold	Plaster	No mold release required.
	Concrete	No mold release required.

Creating a Master

It is easy to create your own mold from a variety of mold-making materials. Molds are made around a master piece – which can be something as small as a button or a piece of jewelry, or it can be a sculpted piece you have made. If you don't already have an item from which you want to make a mold, you will need to create a master. Many projects in this book use natural and found materials such a river rocks, shells, and plastic fruit to make custom molds. You can also try simple sculpting techniques to create unique, creative masters for casting.

Oil-based clay is my material of choice for sculpting masters. It can be found in craft and art supply stores, and an economical substitute is available at toy shops, listed as plasticine. While artists' oil-based clay is finer and nicer to work with, plasticine is an economical substitute that works for novice sculptors.

The casting you make will look like the master. Various objects can be pressed into the clay to form negative details, and found objects can be pushed into the surface of the clay to form positive designs.

Adding texture to a relief sculpture for a mold. This project is the Fruit Plaque. See the Plaster Crafting section for the project instructions.

basic supplies for making a master

- **Oil-based clay,** for sculpting
- **Ceramic tile,** to use as a work surface
- **Sculpting tools** – Roller, detail tools
- **Objects to make indented designs** – rubber stamps, objects with interesting textures
- **Objects to make convex designs** – Pebbles, shells, small castings, etc.
- **Mold-making material,** such as brush-on latex rubber
- **Bowl and hot water,** for softening the clay

step by step

1. **Soften the Clay.**
Put the clay in a plastic bag, seal, and place in a bowl of hot tap water to soften the clay and make it easier to work with.

2. **Form the Base.**
Roll out the clay to a 3/4" to 1" thickness on a ceramic tile. Smooth the top.

3. **Add Texture.**
Texture the surface with a rubber stamp or a textured object.

4. **Add Decorative Elements.**
In this design, a plastic pear, an imprint of leaves, and lettering added with rubber stamps were the decorative elements.

5. **Make the Mold.**
When you are satisfied with the design, make the mold by brushing on the mold material. Allow the mold material to set up. See "Making a Rubber Mold" in this section for more information.

Making a Mold from Polymer Clay

The polymer clay product that is specially designed for making molds is very easy to work with and offers great detail. I prefer to use it for small objects such as buttons, small shells, and pebbles. Molds made from this polymer clay are slightly flexible.

Polymer clay molds can be used for casting regular polymer clay and plaster. I have not had success with pouring resin into them. A pasta machine makes conditioning and rolling out the clay easier and faster. It is a wise investment if you enjoy creating with this medium.

A polymer clay mold. At the left of the mold is a piece of conditioned clay and the gold-color cherub button used as the master. To the right of the mold are two castings made with the mold.

basic supplies for polymer clay molds

- **Polymer clay,** the kind intended for making molds
- **Acrylic roller** or a **pasta machine** used exclusively for polymer clay
- **Polymer clay knife,** for cutting and trimming
- **A ceramic tile,** to use as a working and baking surface
- **A master** Here, I used a small button.

Step by Step

1. Condition the Clay.
Condition and warm the clay well before trying to work with it; as it warms up, it becomes more pliable and easier to work with.

2. Make the Mold.
Form a piece of smoothed and conditioned clay about double the size of the master. Dust the clay lightly with powder or cornstarch to prevent the clay from sticking to your master. Push the master into the piece of clay, and then remove it – leaving the impression.

3. Bake.
Follow the manufacturer's directions carefully for baking the finished mold in your oven. Make sure you have proper ventilation in the room during the baking. Let cool according to the clay manufacturer's instructions. Never bake the master in the clay.

4. Your mold is now ready to use.

Making a Sand Cast Mold

Sand molds have been used for thousands of years to cast metals, and sand is still used for molding a variety of items from delicate jewelry pieces to large machine parts. The process involves pouring molten metal into mold cavities formed out of sand. The finer the sand, the more detail the casting will possess. Sand casting can be done with plaster and cement – rather than metal – to create cast objects for home and garden.

Sand casting mainly is used by novice crafters for casting flat relief pieces. Plaster hand prints and wax candles are two perennially popular sand casting projects for children.

The mold is made from damp sand by pushing in objects to create an impressed design. A sand mold can only be used once, but it is easy and fast to create with found materials. Some sand adheres to the casting; this can be an aesthetic advantage (or not).

Sand is also used as a support for latex, plastic, or natural molds such as the leaf in the Fossil Leaf Fountain project in the Hypertufa Casting section.

basic supplies for sand molds

- **Sand** – Use play box sand or fine masonry sand; both can be found at hardware stores and building supply centers. TIP: If you use sand from a sandbox, sift it through a screen to remove any foreign objects.
- **A large container** to hold the sand. You can use a sandbox or a large plastic container such as a small child's wading pool or a tub.
- **Objects to make impressions** – Almost anything from hands to household objects such as kitchen tools can be used to make impressions. Pencils, pen tops, plastic film cases, game pieces and buttons are just a few ideas. You can add mosaic pieces, mirrors, marbles, shells, and other decorative pieces to your creations.
- **Metal trowel**, for smoothing sand.
- **Casting material** – Plaster or concrete.
- **A stiff brush** – A clean paint brush with stiff bristles works well.
- **A spray bottle** filled with water to spritz the sand as you prepare the mold.

step by step

1. Fill the Container.
Place the clean sand into your container. It should be deep enough to allow you to dig in a shallow impression.

2. Dampen.
Dampen the sand (if you're working outdoors with a large amount, use a water hose). Use enough water to make the sand damp, but not saturated with water. TIP: Have a spray bottle with a fine mist handy to keep the design from crumbling as you work.

3. Make the Mold.
Press objects into the sand to make the mold. If you are not pleased with the design, smooth the sand with a trowel and start again. The bottom of the mold should be flat and smooth and the side walls firm and clear of stray bits of sand.

Photo 1 – Adding the decorative elements to a mold formed in sand. (This project is the Mosaic Mirror Frame in the Plaster Casting section.)

Photo 2 – Brushing the sand from the casted piece.

4. Add Decorative Elements.
The example shows a mirror and mosaic tiles being laid into the carved out sand form. (Photo 1)

5. Mix the Casting Material.
Mix the plaster or concrete according to the package instructions.

6. Pour.
Pour the mixed plaster or concrete into the mold carefully, taking care not to disturb the pattern. TIP: Use a scoop to pour plaster very slowly and close to the sand surface. The sand quickly will draw the moisture away, and the casting will set up quickly.

7. Let Set and Cure.
Let set at least a day, then dig out the casting and allow to continue hardening one more day. Use a stiff bristle brush to brush away the excess sand. (Photo 2) Let cure until completely hardened.

Making a Rubber Mold

Rubber molds offer extreme detail and work with a variety of casting materials. With a rubber mold, you can cast three-dimensional objects – something plastic tray molds cannot do. It takes a bit of time to make a rubber mold, but good results are easy to achieve.

Using Natural Latex

My first choice for making a rubber mold is **natural latex** – it's safe and economical. You can duplicate objects by brushing on layers of latex to create a mold that can be used repeatedly to cast plaster, wax, soap, and casting resins. Because the finished mold is so flexible, it can easily be removed from a cured casting, even with slight undercuts. A rubber mold's flexibility also has a disadvantage – the shape can be distorted if the rubber mold is not contained in a "mother" mold or a **backup support mold**. Small molds do not need a backup mold, but larger, flat molds do.

Synthetic Latex Rubber

You can also use **synthetic latex** to make your mold. It is applied the same way as natural latex. It is usually less expensive (by volume) and colored bright red. It is not, however, as cost efficient as natural latex because it takes twice as much product and time to produce the same mold thickness. The red coloring can come off on some castings, and the level of detail is not as high as that of natural latex.

Silicone Rubber, Urethane Rubber

These two materials are also available for making your own molds, but they are expensive to buy and more complicated to use than latex so I recommend you learn the other forms of mold making before tackling these advanced materials. You can, however, buy silicone and urethane rubber molds in a wide variety of shapes and designs. They produce superior molds and can cast many different materials. Silicone rubber can be used for multiple castings and offers excellent detail.

Plaster or Sand for Backup Support Mold

Backup support molds are usually made of **plaster or sand**. I prefer this combination: I use plaster cloth (strips of gauze covered in plaster that are used to make casts for broken bones, found in craft and art supply stores) to cover the latex mold and provide a stiff backing. Then I place the latex mold with the plaster cloth support into sand for a leveling support.

Step-by-Step

This example uses natural latex.

1. **Prepare.**
Prepare your work surface by placing the master on a clean, smooth ceramic tile.

2. **Brush on Latex Rubber.**
Simply brush a thin coat of liquid rubber over the surface of the master, then around the base to create a 1" flange. (Photo 1) Allow the latex to air dry or use a hair dryer on a warm setting to speed up the drying. *Important:* A thin first layer is best. Avoid a buildup in crevices or puddles – they require extra drying time.

3. **Add Additional Layers.**
When dry, the rubber will have a translucent tan appearance; you can now apply another layer. Allow the combined layers to gradually achieve proper thickness so that there are no weak or thin spots. Make sure each layer is completely dry before adding the next layer. A small piece requires approximately ten coats. For added firmness and support, add a layer of cheesecloth or bandage gauze between your last layers. Let dry.

4. **Release the Master.**
When your mold is dry, dust it lightly with cornstarch or dusting powder and peel the mold off the master. (The cornstarch or powder helps keep the fresh latex from sticking to itself.)

5. **Apply a Mold Release.**
Spray the inside of the mold with a mold release. Turn the mold inside out and use your hands to massage the mold release into the inside of the mold, covering the surfaces completely. Wipe away the excess, turn right side out, and allow the cavity to dry completely before casting. NOTE: **Always** use a mold release when casting with rubber molds. If you don't, the casting could be permanently adhered to the mold.

6. **Support the Mold.**
Support the mold in a small plastic cup by the flange. For larger molds, see the instructions that follow for creating a backup mold.

7. **Cast.**
Pour in the casting material. Let set and cure.

8. **Release and Clean the Casting.**
When the casting is fully cured, simply peel away the mold. (Photo 2)

Photo 1 – Brushing a layer of liquid rubber over a master.

Supporting a Rubber Mold with a Backup Mold

Here's how to make a backup plaster mold for a rubber mold:

1. Create a latex mold, following steps 1, 2, and 3 above, but do not remove it from the master. Let cure until it is completely dry.
2. Cut plaster cloth into strips to cover the latex mold. Cut enough strips to make about 4 to 6 layers, depending on the size of your mold. (Larger molds need more layers.)
3. Dip the plaster cloth in cold water, and let the excess water drip off. Cover the latex mold with the strips, alternating the direction of the strips with each layer. (Photo 4)
4. Let the plaster cloth dry completely (at least 24 hours).
5. When the plaster is dry, lift it off the latex mold. Make sure the latex mold is dry. Sprinkle the latex mold with cornstarch to keep it from sticking to itself. Carefully remove the latex mold from the master.
6. Place the latex mold back in the plaster backup mold. Put in a sand-filled tub. Level to prepare for casting.

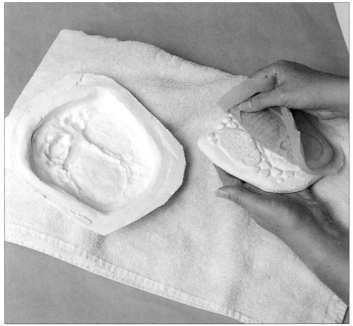

Photo 2 – Peeling a rubber mold off a plaster casting.

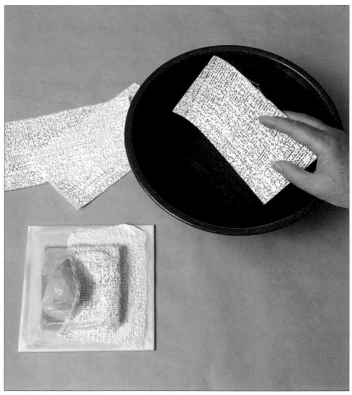

Photo 4 – Applying plaster cloth strips to a rubber mold.

Photo 3 – Four Steps in Casting
Pictured left to right: The master, the rubber mold with backup, the plaster casting, the painted plaster casting.

Clear Casting

techniques & projects

To create clear castings, there are two options – Two-Part Epoxy Casting Resin and Polyester Casting Resin. For epoxy resin casting, exactly equal amounts of the two components, resin and hardener, are mixed together, and the resulting chemical reaction hardens the resin. For polyester resin, a catalyst (hardener) is added to polyester resin to produce a chemical reaction that generates heat and hardens the resin.

The chart on the next page compares the two resins. Choose the one most suitable for your project.

A Tale of Two Resins

Clarity, Maximum/ minimum Pours

- **Epoxy** – It is crystal clear up to a maximum 6-ounce pour with excellent bubble release. Minimum 2-ounce pour.
- **Polyester** – All pours are crystal clear, no bubbles, no maximum pour. However, a 12-ounce maximum pour is recommended for beginners. Minimum 2-ounce pour.

Curing Time

- **Epoxy** – Cures to the touch after 12 hours, may need up to 24 hours before removing from mold.
- **Polyester** – Cures to "click-hard" after approximately 1 hour.

Fumes?

- **Epoxy** – No harsh fumes, user friendly.
- **Polyester** – Strong styrene fumes.

Drilling and Sanding

Both can be drilled or sanded after curing.

- **Epoxy** – If sanded and polished, surface will be frosted in appearance.
- **Polyester** – Can be polished and buffed to a high, glass-like gloss.

Viscosity

- **Epoxy** – Thinner viscosity for detailed casting and better bubble release.
- **Polyester** – Viscosity of corn syrup and light amber or light blue in color. Turns crystal clear after curing.

Pouring Depth

- **Epoxy** – Pours should be 1/4" or deeper, pours under 1/4" take longer to set up.
- **Polyester** – Pours can range from 1/4" to deep pours. Follow the manufacturer's instructions for catalyst/resin ratios for different depth pours.

Mold Releases

- **Epoxy** – Use the mold manufacturer's recommended release for best results in polyethylene and polypropylene molds. Works in rubber latex, urethane, or silicone molds that have been treated with a mold release. *Always* test molds before first use. TIP: Try spot on the backside. See the Supplies section for the test procedure.
- **Polyester** – No release needed when pouring in polyethylene and polypropylene molds. Also works in rubber latex, urethane, or silicone molds that have been treated with a mold release. You can also pour in glass and metal molds; polyester resin shrinks slightly when cured.

Embedding Objects

Many objects can be embedded in both epoxy and polyester resins, such as dried flowers, shells, and buttons. **Never** embed fresh or wet items.

Pouring in Layers

- **Epoxy** – Can be poured in layers in molds without seams or lines.
- **Polyester** – Can be poured in layers in molds without seams or lines while in gel stage; layers cannot be added after one layer is completely cured because polyester shrinks slightly.

Basic Supplies for Resin Casting

Molds

Polypropylene and polyethylene that are manufactured for resin are best. Latex rubber molds and silicone rubber molds also work nicely. Resin jewelry and knob molds come in popular styles and the jewelry pieces match jewelry setting sizes. The molds are smooth and shiny so releasing is easy and castings come out clean and polished looking without extra buffing. With proper care and use of an appropriate mold release, the molds can be used for multiple castings.

Colorants

Use only colorants recommended for use with resins. These universal dyes can be used for polyester casting resin, casting epoxy, and epoxy coatings.

Opaque pigments, transparent dyes, and pearlescent colorants are available. The liquid colorants are high quality, true, clean colors that are excellent for blending and creating numerous designer colors. Opaque pigments impart a solid color; transparent dyes give a clear, transparent coloring. Pigments and dyes can be mixed together.

Tips for Color Mixing:

- *Always* mix your colors on a piece of wax paper before adding them to the resin.
- Use approximately one drop of colorant per ounce of mixed product. Add a drop at a time and mix well to achieve the color concentration you wish.
- A drop of red opaque colorant can be added to white colorant to make a soft pink. Add several drops for a deeper pink hue.
- White will lighten a color, black will darken a color.
- Pearlescent colorants will lighten and add a pearl finish.
- Adding a complementary color will mute the color; for example, a tiny bit of green added to pink will make dusty rose.
- Depending on the size and number of drops, color mixes can vary a great deal. Take notes while mixing colors, especially if making several batches.

Decorative Objects

Items that can be embedded in resin include coins, shells, photos, metal objects such as charms and keys, buttons, and dried flowers. **Never** use fresh flowers or other objects with moisture in them.

Paper Images

Cut motifs from paper, photographs, and stickers can be placed in resin. Non-coated paper must be sealed with two coats of white glue or with a laminating film or the paper will become transparent. Let the sealer coats dry completely before adding to the resin in the mold.

Texture Additives

- **Granite powders**, made from ground, colored resin, are added to casting resins to create realistic-looking granite pieces. Available in a variety of colors, they look white in the powder stage but instantly develop color when added to mixed resin. To use, combine equal amounts granite powder and mixed resin. Mix well.

- **Fibers** such as thread, small pieces of jute string, and (even) strands of hair add fractures and interest in the cast pieces. Add only a small pinch to each mold cavity after a thin layer of mixed resin has been poured.

- **Metallic flakes** such as small pieces of gold, silver, copper, and colored pieces added to mixing cups give a brilliant flash of precious metals.

- **Glitters**, from ultra fine (for dichroic glass) to coarse, can also be used.

- **Iridescent Mylar®** – both flakes, strands, and cut pieces from sheets of iridescent Mylar can be added to mixing cups or mold cavities. They offer bright, interesting effects and are a main component of faux opal and abalone.

- **Beads**, including seed beads, bugle beads, and tiny glass marbles, can also be added to mold cavities. NOTE: It is harder to drill holes or sand cast pieces if glass beads have been added.

- **Fully dried and pressed flowers** can be added to clear resin in the mold cavity; no pre-treatment is necessary. Add **crushed dried herbs and flowers** to the mixing cup for a variety of effects.

- **Polymer clay bits** add texture to castings, and black clay can add realistic details to faux gems such as faux turquoise and jade. To make clay bits, grate polymer clay on a ceramic tile and bake the bits according to the clay manufacturer's directions. Let cool. Add to the mixing cup or the mold cavity.

additives for resin casting

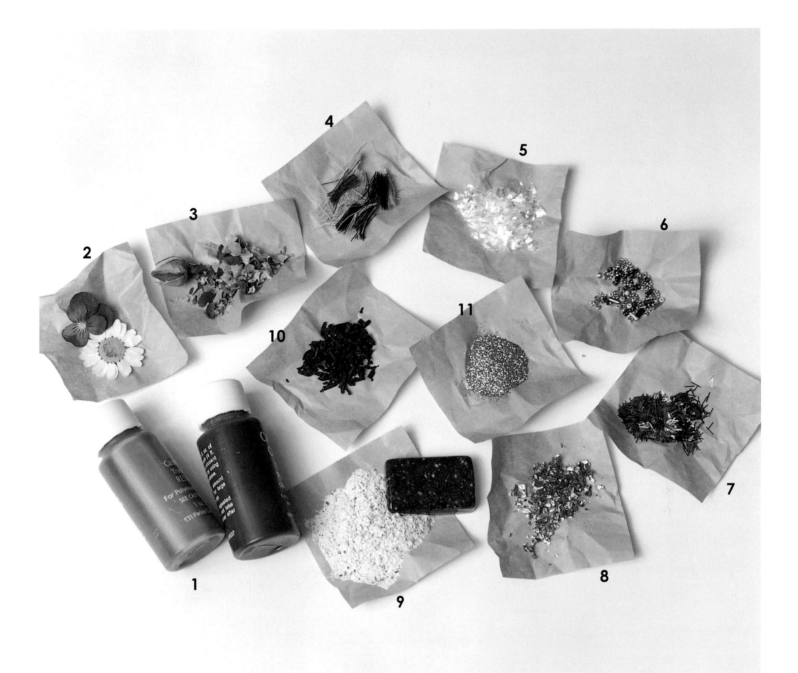

1. Colorants, 2. Pressed dried flowers, 3. Crushed dried flowers, 4. Fibers, 5. Mylar® flakes, 6. Beads, 7. Silver glitter, 8. Metallic flakes, 9. Granite powder, 10. Polymer clay bits, 11. Fine glitter

Polyester Resin Casting

Polyester resin allows you to cast crystal-clear plastic shapes. You can embed objects in the resin to create unique memory pieces. In its liquid form, polyester resin has a consistency of corn syrup and has light amber or light blue coloring. During the hardening process the resin becomes crystal clear. Because one disadvantage of polyester resin is its objectionable styrene odor, good ventilation is a high priority.

It is important to correctly calculate the ratio of catalyst to resin. Generally, the higher volume of resin, the less catalyst you add. For example, if you wish to create faux water in a vase that will hold 8 ounces of resin and be 3" deep, you would add one drop of catalyst per ounce. If you are pouring the same 8 ounces of resin into a large mold and it will be only 1/4" deep, you would add 8 drops of catalyst per ounce. The amount of catalyst also changes if you are pouring a single layer casting or a multiple layer casting. *Important:* **Always** refer to the catalyst chart on the container and follow the manufacturer's recommendations. All the polyester catalyst/resin ratios for the projects in this section are approximations only.

It's also important to consider the temperature and humidity of your work area. My catalyst/resin ratios are calculated for work areas that are 60 to 75 degrees F. without excessive humidity. Check the manufacturer's recommendations regarding cooler or warmer environments.

Store casting resin at room temperature, out of direct sunlight and out of the reach of children. When stored properly, the shelf life of polyester resin is nine to twelve months.

basic supplies for polyester resin

- **Polyester casting resin**

- **Catalyst**, sold alongside or with the resin

- **Additives**, such as objects to embed or additives for texture

- **Resin colorants**, for tinting

- **Mold** – Polypropylene and polyethylene molds manufactured for polyester resins are best. Latex rubber molds and silicone rubber molds also work nicely.

- **Mold release** if using a latex rubber or silicone molds

- **Curing agent** (also called air dry wax) – *You will need this if the last layer of the casting is colored.* This additive creates a film on the top of the casting for proper curing and to avoid sticky areas on the finished casting. **Never** add a curing agent if your intention is a clear casting – it will cloud the resin.

- **Plastic cling wrap** – *You will need this if the casting is clear.*
  Household plastic wrap can be used to seal a clear casting after pouring to prevent sticky spots on the cured resin piece. Simply cover the top of the mold with plastic wrap – but don't let it touch the resin – to create an air-free curing environment.

- **Equipment – You will need the following for each project:**
  Mixing cups – Use disposable plastic cups with graduated measurements
  Wooden stir stick, for stirring
  Disposable glue brush, for brushing the objects before placing them to avoid air bubbles
  Latex gloves, to protect your hands
  Freezer paper, to protect your work surface

polyester resin casting, step by step

The Universe Gazing Paperweight is used as the example for this technique.

In addition to the Basic Supplies for every project listed on page 26, you will need:

• Dome mold, 4 oz. capacity
• Iridescent fibers, metallic flakes, fine glitter
• Black colorant

1. Determine the Capacity of Mold.

The dome mold has a capacity of 4. oz. If your mold does not have the capacity printed on it, you can easily determine the capacity of the mold. Simply fill with water and pour into a measuring cup. Dry the mold completely before using.

2. Measure the Resin for Your First Pour.

Determine the amount and depth of your first pour. Place the appropriate number of ounces of resin in the mixing cup. Following the manufacturer's instructions, calculate the amount of catalyst for the pour. Holding the bottle straight up and down, add the number of drops of catalyst needed. It is important to be precise to ensure proper curing. For the first pour of this project, I used 3 ounces of resin and 4 drops of catalyst for the first pour. (Photo 1)

3. Mix the Resin for Your First Pour.

Using the stir stick, mix the resin and catalyst thoroughly and vigorously for 1 minute. Scrape the sides and bottom of the cup with the stir stick to ensure proper mixing.

4. Pour the Resin into the Mold.

Make sure the mold is level. Pour the mixed resin into the mold. Do not pick up or move the mold after you have poured the resin.

5. Let the Resin Gel.

It will take 15 to 25 minutes. Test the surface with a stir stick. At this point is when you should add your decorative objects you want imbedded into your piece.

6. Place Additives.

When the resin is in the gel stage, add the additives – the gel should support their weight. In this case, I'm adding fibers, flakes, and glitter. (Photo 2)

TIPS:
• Place objects upside down and in reverse.
• When embedding an item that may trap air bubbles, dip or coat the object with some catalyzed resin before placing it face down on the gelled surface. Gently press with a stir stick to help free any trapped bubbles.

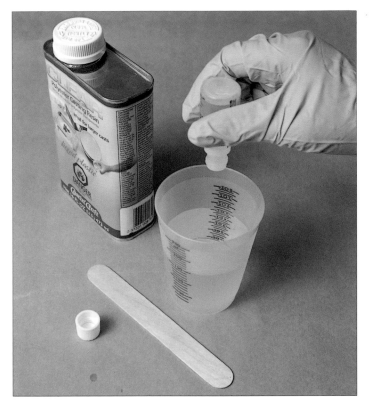

Photo 1 – Adding catalyst to resin in the mixing cup.

Photo 2 – Placing additives on the first layer.

Polyester Resin Casting Continued from page 27

7. Mix and Pour the Second Layer.

For this project, I mixed 1 ounce of resin, 3 drops of catalyst, black colorant, and (because this is a colored layer) a surface-curing agent. Pour the second layer (in this case it's the final layer) of resin into the mold. (Photo 3)

8. Allow Piece to Cure.

The casting will be "click hard" (if you tap it with your fingernail) and the edges will have pulled away from the sides of the mold when the casting is cured. This can take from 1 hour to up to 24 hours. If the surface remains tacky, allow up to several days to harden.

9. Remove from the Mold.

Remove the casting from the mold by flexing the mold slightly, as you would an ice cube tray. The casting should drop out of the mold easily.

10. Finish.

Although it is not generally necessary, the casting can be polished with rubbing compound or sprayed with a clear acrylic spray to remove blemishes or fingerprints. *Option:* Add a piece of felt or cork to the bottom.

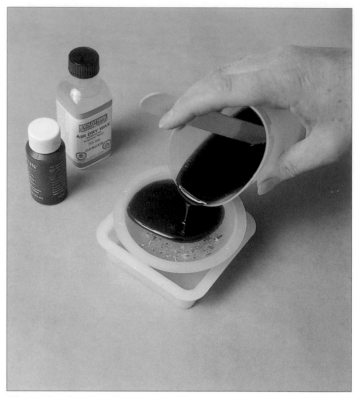

Photo 3 – Pouring the second layer.

Photo 4 – Removing the paperweight from the mold.

Vintage Pen Holder

When giving this project as a gift, choose metal letters that are the initials of your intended recipient.

supplies

- Polyester casting resin, 9 ounces
- Resin catalyst
- Rectangular resin mold, 3" x 6" x 1-1/16" deep, 9 ounce capacity
- Black colorant
- Objects to imbed – Coins, laminated stamps, laminated postcard, metal keys, metal lettering embellishments, pen nibs
- Finishing embellishments – Pen and holder, measuring tape ribbon, thin cork sheet
- White craft glue
- 30-minute epoxy glue
- Equipment from list of Basic Supplies (See page 26.)

instructions

Pour:

This casting was done in three layers. Each layer contains approximately 3 ounces resin and was poured 3/8" deep.

1. First layer – Use 4 drops catalyst and 3 ounces resin. Mix and pour, then let gel. When gelled, add the coins, keys, pen nibs and metal letters.
2. Second layer – Use 3 drops catalyst and 3 ounces resin. Mix and pour, then let gel. When gelled, add the paper objects. To prevent bubbles, brush the laminated paper pieces with catalyzed resin before placing face down on the first layer.
3. Third (final) layer – Use 2 drops catalyst and 3 ounces resin. Add 3 to 4 drops opaque black colorant. Mix and pour. Let cure.

Finish:

4. Remove casting from mold.
5. Adhere the pen holder to the top of the casting with 30-minute epoxy.
6. Glue cork sheet cut to fit on the bottom, using white craft glue.
7. Glue measuring tape ribbon around the edge, using white craft glue. ❏

Tea Time Recipe Holder

This casting holds teatime treasures, including an unused tea bag, a tiny glass vial filled with tea leaves, and an oval label holder holding a piece of laminated paper and a mini spoon charm.

supplies

- Polyester casting resin, 8 ounces
- Resin catalyst
- Rectangular resin mold, 3" x 5" x 1-1/16" deep, 8 ounce capacity
- Amber colorant
- Objects to imbed – Tea bag and spoon charms, oval label holder, laminated tea label, real (unused) tea bag, green silk leaves, corked mini glass vial filled with tea leaves, metal letters to spell T-E-A
- Finishing embellishments – 1" wide brown satin ribbon, crown place card holder, cork sheeting
- White craft glue
- 30-minute epoxy glue
- Equipment from list of Basic Supplies (See page 26.)

instructions

Pour:

This casting was poured in three layers. Each layer contains approximately 2-1/2 ounces of resin and is 3/8" deep.

1. First layer – Use 4 drops catalyst and 2-1/2 ounces resin. Mix and pour, then let gel. When gelled, add the charms, label holder, glass vial, and metal letters.
2. Second layer – Use 3 drops catalyst and 2-1/2 ounces resin. Mix and pour, then let gel. When gelled, add the paper label, tea bag, and silk leaves. Brush the pieces with catalyzed resin before placing face down on the first layer to prevent bubbles.
3. Third (final) layer – Use 2 drops catalyst and 2 ounces resin. Add 2 to 3 drops transparent amber colorant. Mix and pour. Let cure.

Finish:

4. Remove casting from mold.
5. Attach the place card holder to the top of the casting with 30-minute epoxy glue.
6. Glue cork sheet cut to size on the bottom, using white craft glue.
7. Glue ribbon around the edge, using white craft glue. ❏

Memory Bricks

These castings display old photographs embellished with charms and vintage buttons. Photocopy your photograph and use the copy for the casting to preserve the original. Look for embellishments in crafts stores and where scrapbooking supplies are sold.

supplies

- Polyester casting resin, 15 ounces (for three memory bricks)
- Resin catalyst
- Square resin mold, 3" x 3" x 1-1/16" deep, 5 ounce capacity
- Black colorant
- Objects to imbed – Metal heart charms, laminated photographs, mother of pearl buttons
- Finishing embellishments – 1/2" wide pink and brown ribbons, mother of pearl buttons, label holders, fleur de lis copper charms
- White craft glue
- 30-minute epoxy glue
- Equipment from list of Basic Supplies (See page 26.)

instructions

NOTE: These instructions are for making one casting.

Pour:

This casting was done in three layers. Each layer contains approximately 1-1/2 ounces resin and is 3/8" deep.

1. First layer – Use 5 drops catalyst and 1-1/2 ounces resin. Mix and pour, then let gel. When gelled, add the metallic heart and buttons.
2. Second layer – Use 4 drops catalyst and 1-1/2 ounces resin. Mix and pour, then let gel. When gelled, add the laminated photographs. To prevent bubbles, brush the photographs with catalyzed resin before placing face down on the first layer.
3. Third (final) layer – Use 3 drops catalyst and 1-1/2 ounces resin. Add 2 to 3 drops opaque black colorant. Mix and pour. Let cure.

Finish:

4. Remove casting from mold.
5. Attach the label holder and charm to the top of the casting with 30-minute epoxy glue.
6. Glue the ribbon and buttons around the edge, using white craft glue.
7. *Option:* Add a paper backing for writing information about the photograph(s), such as names and dates. ❏

Memories Paperweight

This charming paperweight is a perfect gift for a parent's desk. Here, a lock of Samantha's curly hair was tied with a bow and embedded with her photograph. (In the resin, the hair lost a bit of its curl and looks darker than it actually is.)

supplies

- Polyester casting resin, 4 ounces
- Resin catalyst
- Dome resin mold, 3" diameter, 1-3/8" deep, 4 ounce capacity
- White colorant
- Objects to imbed – Laminated photograph, letter beads strung on a piece of pink wire, (optional) lock of hair with tiny bow
- Finishing embellishments – Self-adhesive cork dots for bottom
- Equipment from list of Basic Supplies (See page 26.)

instructions

Pour:

This casting was done in three layers. Each layer contains approximately 1 ounce resin and is a little less than 1/2" deep.

1. First layer – Use 5 drops catalyst and 1 ounce resin. Mix and pour, then let gel. When gelled, add the letter beads and lock of hair.
2. Second layer – Use 4 drops catalyst and 1 ounce resin. Mix and pour, then let gel. When gelled, add the laminated photograph. To prevent bubbles, brush the photograph with catalyzed resin before placing face down on the first layer.
3. Third (final) layer – Use 3 drops catalyst and 1 ounce resin. Add 2 to 3 drops opaque white colorant. Mix and pour. Let cure.

Finish:

4. Remove casting from mold.
5. Attach the cork dots to the bottom. ❏

Fish Paperweight

A little toy goldfish caught swimming in clear resin makes a colorful, friendly paperweight.
My little fish had a hollow center and expelled a tiny bubble just as the resin gelled – an effect
I'm not sure I could duplicate! Find the coral sand and shells at pet and aquarium supply stores.

supplies

- Polyester casting resin, 4 ounces
- Resin catalyst
- Dome resin mold, 3" diameter x 1-3/8" deep, 4 ounce capacity
- Blue colorant
- Objects to imbed – Toy goldfish, shells, coral sand, dried starfish
- Finishing embellishments – Self-adhesive clear plastic dots for bottom
- Equipment from list of Basic Supplies (See page 26.)

instructions

Pour:

This casting was done in two layers. Each layer contains approximately 1-1/2 ounces resin. The first is 1" deep; the second is 3/8" deep.

1. First layer – Use 5 drops catalyst and 1-1/2 ounces resin. Mix and pour, then let gel slightly. Add the fish, pressing it into the semi-set gel. Make sure the fish stays upright as the resin continues to gel and becomes firm enough to add the shells, starfish, and coral sand.
2. Second and final layer – Use 4 drops catalyst and 1-1/2 ounces resin. Add 2 to 3 drops transparent blue colorant. Mix and pour. Let cure.

Finish:

3. Remove casting from mold.
4. Attach the clear dots to the bottom. ❑

Epoxy Resin Casting

Epoxy casting resin is a good choice for casting small objects. It's comprised of two parts, a resin and a hardener. When equal amounts of resin and hardener are mixed together, a chemical reaction causes heat, which cures and hardens the resin. Epoxy casting resin can be used to glue jewelry findings for a strong hold. For a quicker bond, use 30-minute epoxy glue.

epoxy resin casting, basic supplies

- **Two-part epoxy casting resin**
- **Additives,** such as objects to embed or additives for decoration or texture.
- **Resin colorants,** for tinting
- **Mold** – follow the chart to choose the best mold for this material
- **Mold release agent** – choose the type that is right for the mold you are using
- **Equipment – You will need the following for each project:**
  Mixing cups – Disposable graduated plastic cups
  Wooden stir stick, for mixing
  Disposable glue brush, for brushing the objects before placing to avoid air bubbles.
  Latex gloves, to protect your hands.
  Freezer paper or wax paper, to protect your work surface.
  Paper towels, for wiping
  Sandpaper, 150-grit, for polishing. *Optional:* Rotary sanding tool
  Car wax or carnauba wax, for polishing

epoxy resin casting, step by step – the two-cup method

Follow these steps when using two-part epoxy casting resin. IMPORTANT: Read through the instructions and be sure you have all the materials and equipment ready before you start. Cover your work area with freezer paper or wax paper.

1. **Condition the Mold.**
Spray the mold with mold release. Using a clean paper towel, wipe the entire mold to remove excess moisture. (Photo 1) Set aside to dry.

2. **Warm the Epoxy Casting Resin.**
Warming the resin and hardener before measuring ensures even mixing and minimal bubbles.
Fill a small bowl with warm, **not hot,** tap water. (Warm means you can put your hand in the water without discomfort. If the water is too hot, the casting resin will set up too quickly.) Place the bottles in the water for 10 minutes. Remove and wipe dry with a paper towel.

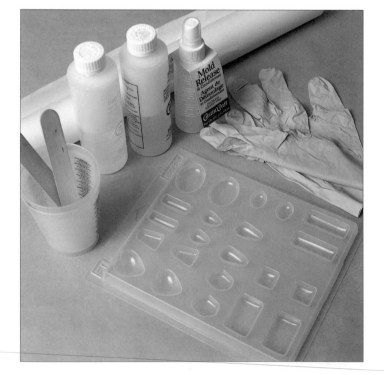

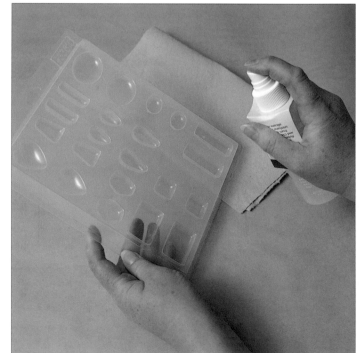

Photo 1 – Conditioning the mold.

3. Measure the Resin.

Use a marker to label the measuring/mixing cups #1 and #2. Estimate the amount of resin needed to make the project, using the mold capacity as a guide. Measure equal amounts of hardener and resin in container #1. (Photo 2) **Do not guess** – the measurements must be exact or the castings will not harden properly.

TIPS:
- Mix only what you need. You cannot save mixed resin for a second pour.
- You need to mix a minimum of 2 ounces (1 ounce resin, 1 ounce hardener) – plan to fill an entire tray mold rather than just one or two cavities.

4. Mix the Resin in Container #1.

Mix the hardener and the resin together well for a full 2 minutes. Scrape the sides and the stir stick often to ensure you are mixing completely. If you are using colorant, add it now. Mix well for an additional 30 seconds.

5. Pour into Container #2.

Pour the mixed resin from container #1 into container #2. Scrape the resin off the inside of container #1 and the stir stick. Mix the resin in container #2 for 1 minute. If you are including decorative additives, add them to container #2 now. Mix for an additional 30 seconds or longer, until incorporated. (Photo 3)

6. Pour into Mold.

Pour the resin into the prepared mold(s), using the stir stick to control the flow into the mold cavities. (Photo 4) Don't worry if you drip the mixed resin on the mold – it will come off easily when hardened. Discard the mixing containers and the stir stick.

7. Let Resin Cure.

If, after 10 minutes, there are bubbles on the surface or the resin, remove them by gently passing a hot hair dryer on the low blower setting over the mold or by blowing on them gently through a straw. Let cure and harden. This will take from 4 to 12 hours, depending on the room temperature. For best results, allow to cure overnight.

8. Remove from the Mold.

When the resin is completely cured, gently press the back of the mold with your thumbs and tap out the cured pieces.

9. Sand the Back of the Casting.

Sand off the edges of the cast pieces, using a piece of 150-grit sandpaper or the sanding attachment on a rotary tool. Keep the casting at a 45-degree angle to the surface of the sandpaper to prevent marring the surface.

10. Polish.

Rub car wax or carnauba wax on the casting to help eliminate the sanded white edge and protect your cast pieces from scratches.

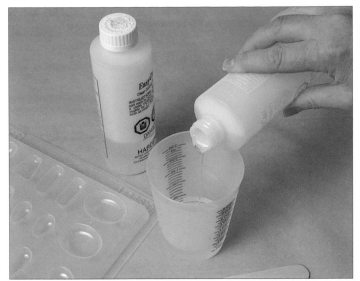
Photo 2 – Measuring the resin and hardener.

Photo 3 – Stirring additives during the second mixing.

Photo 4 – Pouring mixed resin into a tray mold.

Layering with Epoxy Casting Resin

Use this technique for imbedding objects in a cast piece or for creating special effects, such as dichroic glass.

instructions

1. Mix the epoxy resin according to the step-by-step instructions for the two-cup method.
2. Pour a 1/4" layer of clear resin at the bottom of the mold. Remove any bubbles.
3. To prevent bubbles, brush the object(s) you wish to imbed with a coat of resin, then place the object(s) in the still-liquid resin. Let cure and harden.
4. Mix the second resin layer, using the same mixing procedure you used for the first layer and adding colorants, glitter, or other additives. Pour into the mold. Let cure and unmold.

Puddle Beads

This technique is a great way to produce matching beads for your cast pieces – just save a small amount of mixed resin from your casting and pour it in a puddle. When the resin puddle is set up but still flexible, it can be cut into strips and rolled to make beads.
By varying the strip size, the additives, and the thickness of the puddle, the bead possibilities are endless. You can make dozens of clear or translucent beads easily and quickly.

instructions

1. Pour 2 ounces of mixed resin on freezer paper. Spread two thin 10" x 5" puddles with the wooden stir stick. The thickness of the puddle determines the thickness of the beads – pour a thicker puddle for thicker beads, a thinner puddle for thinner beads.
2. Sprinkle decorative materials on the resin. Let cure 8 to 12 hours. (After this time, the puddle can be handled, but is still flexible.)
3. Using scissors, cut the puddle into strips. A 1" x 4" strip will make a 1" long bead about 1/2" thick.
4. Roll each strip to create a cylindrical bead with a hole in the center. Use masking tape to secure the end of the strip. Allow to cure 12 hours.

Option: Cut the strips into long triangles to create cone-shaped beads. ❑

Rolling puddle beads from strips of semi-set resin.

Finishing Techniques

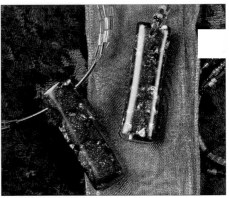

Photo 1 – Holes are drilled into these two faux gems so that they can be attached to a necklace.

Drilling

It's easy to drill a hole in epoxy castings using a hand drill or a rotary tool. Use a 1/8" or smaller drill bit for jewelry pieces.

1. Mark the hole with a black marker.
2. Drill. When drilling a deep hole, pull back on the drill to let the resin shavings fall out of the hole. If you don't, the drill can seize up and stop.
3. Polish the insides of drilled holes with a chenille stem coated with a little carnauba wax to remove the white surface.

Adding Jewelry Findings & Knob Hardware

Epoxy resin can be used to glue jewelry findings and hardware to the backs of cast pieces.

1. Mix 2 ounces of resin (1 ounce resin, 1 ounce hardener).
2. Use a glue brush or toothpick to apply the mixed resin to the back of the cast piece. Press the hardware or findings in place.

Option: You can use a 30-minute epoxy glue for a quicker bond on jewelry pieces, but use epoxy casting resin for gluing knob hardware for a super strong hold.

Photo 2 – Epoxy was used to glue the jewelry findings to the pendants.

Placing Embedded Findings

Embedded findings are both useful and decorative. While you are creating a casting for a piece of jewelry, you can place findings in the still-uncured resin if they can be supported by the mold. (If they aren't supported by the mold, they'll sink to the bottom.) For example, 1" long metallic tube beads can be placed over the cavity and into the resin. When cured, you have a built-in finding that you can now thread. You can also form wire to make custom findings for small pieces and embed them.

Adding Charms & Small Resin Pieces

Charms and smaller cast resin pieces can be added to the surface of a cast piece for dimensional effects. To adhere, use a small amount of mixed resin or 30-minute epoxy. Apply with a toothpick.

Photo 3 – A coin is glued to the front of the resin cabinet knob using a small amount of mixed liquid resin.

Laminating Pieces Together

Here's how to make a three-dimensional piece, such as a heart pendant:

1. Fill two heart cavities in a mold with mixed resin. Let cure.
2. Remove one of the cast pieces from the mold.
3. Pour a small amount of mixed resin on top of the second cast piece (the one still in the mold).
4. Place the first heart casting on top, flat sides together. Let cure. *Option:* Sandwich a piece of wire or a jewelry finding between the two castings to create a built-in finding.
5. When cured, unmold the piece. Sand and polish the seam.

Photo 4 – Two heart pieces were laminated together with a head pin between to create this heart pendant.

Making Faux Gems

Use these recipes to make faux gems from resin.

Dichroic Glass

1. Pour a thin layer of clear mixed resin into the mold cavity.
2. Add metallic flakes, Mylar® pieces, or ultra fine glitter. (You can also use a combination of all three.) Let cure.
3. Top up the cavity with a layer of colored mixed resin. Use black for a dramatic effect or a transparent color for a glass-like effect.

Amber

1. To the mixing cup, add amber tint, a few drops at a time until you reach your desired shade.
2. Add a pinch of crushed, dried rose petals, a pinch of copper metallic flakes, and a pinch of gold metallic flakes. Mix well.
3. Pour into the mold cavities.
4. Sprinkle a few pieces of black polymer clay bits into each cavity. Let cure.

For fossil amber, add plastic ants (found at toy stores) or dry, dead bugs that have naturally passed away on your window ledge to the clear mix in the mold cavity.

Jade

1. To the mixing cup, add transparent green and amber tints, a few drops at a time until you reach your desired shade. *Option:* Add a tiny drop of white opaque pigment for a semi-translucent jade piece. Mix well.
2. Pour into the mold cavities.
3. Sprinkle a few pieces of black polymer clay bits into each cavity. Let cure.

Rose Quartz

1. To the mixing cup, add transparent red and pearlescent colorants for a light pink hue, a few drops at a time until you reach your desired shade.
2. Add a pinch of gold metallic flakes. Mix well.
3. Pour into the mold cavities.
4. Mix a little resin with white opaque pigment. Add a few drops to each cavity. Gently swirl in with a toothpick. Let cure.

Turquoise

1. To the mixing cup, add blue and white tints for a light blue hue, a few drops at a time until you reach your desired shade. Add a tiny touch of amber colorant to mute the blue.
2. Add a pinch of black polymer bits. Mix well.
3. Pour into the mold cavities. Let cure.

Opal

1. Pour a thin layer of clear mixed resin into the mold cavity.
2. Add iridescent Mylar® flakes or a cut piece of Mylar® sheet. Let cure.
3. Top up the cavity with a white layer of mixed resin colored with white opaque pigment. For variety, add a top layer of transparent tinted resin to create colored opal gems.

Abalone

1. Pour a thin layer of clear mixed resin into the mold cavity.
2. Add iridescent Mylar® flakes or a cut piece of Mylar® sheet. Let cure.
3. Top up the cavity with a black layer of mixed resin colored with black opaque pigment.

Rutilated Quartz

1. To the mixing cup, add amber colorant, a few drops at a time until you reach your desired shade.
2. Pour into the mold cavity, filling it 3/4 full.
3. Add a variety of thin fibers to each cavity. (Gold and brown threads work well.) Let cure.
4. Top each cavity with a layer of golden tan resin (colored with amber tint and white pigment). Let cure.

Fantasy Glass

Add Mylar® fibers and flakes to colored resin. Experiment with colorants for a rainbow of hues.

1. Jade
2. Turquoise
3. Rose quartz
4. Dichroic Glass
5. Opal
6. Abalone
7. Amber
8. Rutilated quartz
9. Fantasy glass
10. Paper object
11. Mini collage
12. Granite powder

Basic Beading

Basic beading techniques using glass beads, crimp beads, and flexible jewelry cords and wires were used to create the jewelry projects. Basic equipment for beading includes:
• Crimping pliers
• Wire cutters
• Needlenose jewelry pliers
• Beading mat or tray.

Jewelry Lengths

For necklaces and bracelets, you can decide the length of your finished piece. Standard lengths, in inches, are:

• Choker: 15-16"
• Princess necklace: 18-20"
• Matinee necklace: 23-27"
• Opera necklace: 30-32"
• Bracelet: 7"
• Anklet: 9-10"

Frosted "Glass" Pendants

To make these necklaces, I poured clear epoxy resin into a push mold that was designed for polymer clay. The castings have a frosted, matte surface that looks like frosted glass. Both pieces were made using the same technique, but the beading patterns are different.

supplies

Two-part epoxy casting resin

Polymer clay push mold – Face motif

Mold release (PVA or silicone-base)

Silver jewelry disks, oval and round

1" long silver tube beads

Beads – Clear bugle beads, star beads, clear E beads, opalescent glass chip beads

10 ft. silver beading cable

2 silver toggle clasps

4 crimping beads and crimping tool

30-minute epoxy glue

Equipment from list of Basic Supplies. (See page 36.)

instructions

Make the Casting:

1. Mix clear resin and pour into a prepared face motif push mold. Let cure.
2. Release from mold. Sand the edges.

Make the Pendants:

3. Glue each casting on a silver disk with a silver tube bead at the top, using 30-minute epoxy. Let set.

Assemble the Necklaces:

4. Cut four 28" lengths of beading cable, two for each necklace. Run two lengths through each tube bead on the pendants.
5. String 9" of beads on each side of both pendants.
6. Attach the silver toggle clasps by running the beading cable through the clasp end and back through a crimp bead. Crimp the bead to secure. Thread the cable end through a few beads. Trim any excess. Repeat on the other side. Repeat on the other necklace. ❑

"Glass Bead" Necklace

This simple design yields dramatic results. The puddle bead technique is used to create the cylindrical glass-like beads.

supplies

Two-part epoxy casting resin

Gold metallic flakes

Beads – 13 to 15, 10 mm gold corrugated beads, 13 to 15, 6 mm gold spacer disk beads

Clear elastic beading cord

Equipment from list of Basic Supplies. (See page 36.)

instructions

1. Following the instructions for puddle beads located earlier in this section, create 13 to 15, 1" long cylinder beads. Sprinkle gold metallic flakes into the resin puddle for the golden bits. Let cure.

2. Thread the resin cylinder beads, the gold beads, and disk beads on clear beading cord.

3. To finish, tie the ends of the beading cord in a square knot. Add a drop of mixed resin to secure the knot. Let cure fully before use. ❑

Faux Amber Pendants

I made latex molds from river stones and used them to cast these "amber" pendants.
A cast piece made in a latex mold will have a slight matte finish. For a glossy finish,
coat the casting with clear resin after releasing it from the mold. That's what
I did to the elongated pendant in this trio.

supplies

Two-part epoxy casting resin

Latex mold made from river rocks (See
"Making a Rubber Mold.")

Mold release

Faux amber additives – Amber
colorant, gold and copper metallic
flakes, crushed dried roses, black
polymer clay bits

Beads – Amber chip beads, brown,
amber, copper and gold seed beads,
15 mm oval amber glass beads

6 yds. gold beading cable

3 gold toggle clasps

6 gold crimping beads and crimping
tool

Drill and 1/8" drill bit

Wire cutters

Equipment from list of Basic Supplies.
(See page 36.)

instructions

Make the Castings:

1. Mix the resin with the amber additives,
   following the instructions for "Making
   Faux Gems."
2. Pour into the latex molds. Let cure.
3. Release from the molds. Sand and polish
   the edges.
4. Using a 1/8" drill bit, drill a hole in the
   top of each amber cast piece. Polish
   inside the holes.

Assemble the Necklaces:

5. Cut six 36" lengths of beading cable.
   Using the photo as a guide, thread the
   cable strands through the holes in the
   pendants.
6. Using the photo as a guide, add beads to
   the cables for 12" on each side to create
   matinee-length necklaces.
7. Attach the gold toggle clasps by running
   each end of the beading cables through
   the clasp end and back through a crimp

bead. Crimp the bead to secure. Thread
the remaining cable through the beads
near the end and trim any excess cable.
Repeat on the other side. Repeat to
complete the other two necklaces. ❏

"Amber" Heart Pendant & Bracelet

The heart pendant is cast using the faux amber technique. The two cast pieces are laminated to form a three-dimensional piece. Paired with black glass and gold beads, it makes a gorgeous necklace. The cast pieces of the bracelet are connected with elastic cording and separated with black and gold beads.

HEART PENDANT

supplies for heart pendant

Two-part epoxy casting resin

Jewelry mold with heart cavities

Mold release

Faux amber additives – Amber colorant, gold and copper metallic flakes, crushed dried roses, black polymer clay bits

Beads – Black glass chip beads, gold metallic E beads

24" gold beading cable

1 gold toggle clasp

2 gold crimping beads and crimping tool

Gold wire head pin

Wire cutters

Equipment from list of Basic Supplies. (See page 36.)

instructions for heart pendant

Make the Castings:

1. Mix resin with amber additives. Pour into the cavities of a prepared heart mold. Let cure.
2. Remove the cast pieces from the mold. Laminate the flat sides together, following the instructions for "Laminating Pieces Together" to form a three-dimensional heart pendant with a wire head pin sandwiched between them. Let cure.
3. Sand the seam. Polish.

Assemble the Necklace:

4. Slip the 24" length of beading cable through the head pin. Thread 8" of beads on each side to create a princess-length necklace.
5. Attach the gold toggle clasp by running the beading cable on one side through one side of the clasp and back through a crimp bead. Crimp the bead to secure. Thread the cable end through the beads near the end and trim excess cable. Repeat on the other side. ❏

BRACELET

supplies for bracelet

Two-part epoxy casting resin

Jewelry mold with large rectangular cavities

Mold release

Faux amber additives – Amber colorant, gold and copper metallic flakes, crushed dried roses, black polymer clay bits

Beads – Black 5 mm crystal beads, gold metallic 5 mm beads

1 yd. clear elastic beading cord

Drill and 1/8" drill bit

Equipment from list of Basic Supplies. (See page 36.)

instructions for bracelet

Make the Castings:

1. Mix the resin with the amber additives. Pour into the prepared mold cavities – you need to make five rectangular pieces. Let cure.
2. Release the pieces from the mold. Sand and polish the edges.
3. Mark and drill three holes on the side of each piece. Polish inside each drilled hole.

Assemble the Bracelet:

4. Cut the beading cord into three 12" pieces. Thread the cast pieces on the beading cord, placing beads between each piece.
5. Tie the ends of the cord in square knots. Add a drop of mixed resin to secure the knots. Let cure fully before using. ❏

Faux Dichroic Pendants

Both these necklaces started with pendants made in the same-size molds, but they were finished with different techniques – one was drilled with a hole; a finding was embedded in the other.

supplies

Two-part epoxy casting resin

Jewelry mold with narrow rectangular cavities

Mold release

Dichroic additives – Black colorant, iridescent flakes, colored glitter

Beads – Gold bugle beads, multi-colored seed beads, 5 mm black crystal beads, one 1" gold metallic tube bead

5 yds. gold beading cable

2 gold toggle clasps

4 gold crimping beads and crimping tool

Wire cutters

Drill and 1/8" drill bit

Equipment from list of Basic Supplies. (See page 36.)

instructions

Make the Castings:

See the instructions for "Making Faux Gems."

1. Mix resin with dichroic additives and pour into the prepared narrow rectangular cavities of the mold. Embed one casting with a 1" gold metallic tube bead. Let cure.
2. Release from the molds. Sand and polish the edges.
3. Using a 1/8" drill bit, drill a hole in the casting without the embedded tube bead.

Assemble the Necklaces:

4. Cut six 30" lengths of beading cable. Thread three through each casting.
5. Using the photo as a guide, bead 12" on both sides of each pendant to create two matinee-length necklaces.
6. Attach the gold toggle clasps by running the beading cables on one side of one necklace through one side of a clasp end and back through a crimp bead. Crimp the bead to secure. Thread the remaining cable through the beads at that end and trim any excess. Repeat with the other side. Repeat with the other necklace. ❏

Oval "Dichroic" Pendant

I glued this cast pendant into a jewelry finding. The shape of the jewelry mold I used corresponds with standard jewelry findings.

supplies

Two-part epoxy casting resin

Jewelry mold with large oval cavity

Mold release

Dichroic additives – Black colorant, iridescent flakes, colored glitter

Beads – Gold bugle beads, gold E beads, 8 mm black iridescent crystal beads

30-minute epoxy glue

30" gold beading cable

Gold oval bezel with finding

1 gold toggle clasp

2 gold crimping beads

Equipment from list of Basic Supplies. (See page 36.)

instructions

Make the Casting:

See the instructions for "Making Faux Gems."

1. Mix resin with dichroic additives and pour into the prepared large oval cavity of the mold. Let cure.
2. Release from the mold. Sand and polish the edges.
3. Glue the cast piece into the gold jewelry bezel with 30-minute epoxy glue. Let set.

Make the Necklace:

4. Place the bezel with the casting at the center of the beading cable.
5. Add 12" of beads on each side to create a matinee-length necklace.
6. Attach the gold toggle clasp by running one end of the beading cable through one side of the clasp and back through a crimping bead. Crimp the bead to secure. Thread the remaining cable through the beads at that end and trim the excess. Repeat on the other side. ❏

Pictured top to bottom: Oval Dichroic Pendant Necklace, Necklaces with Faux Dichroic Rectangular Pendants

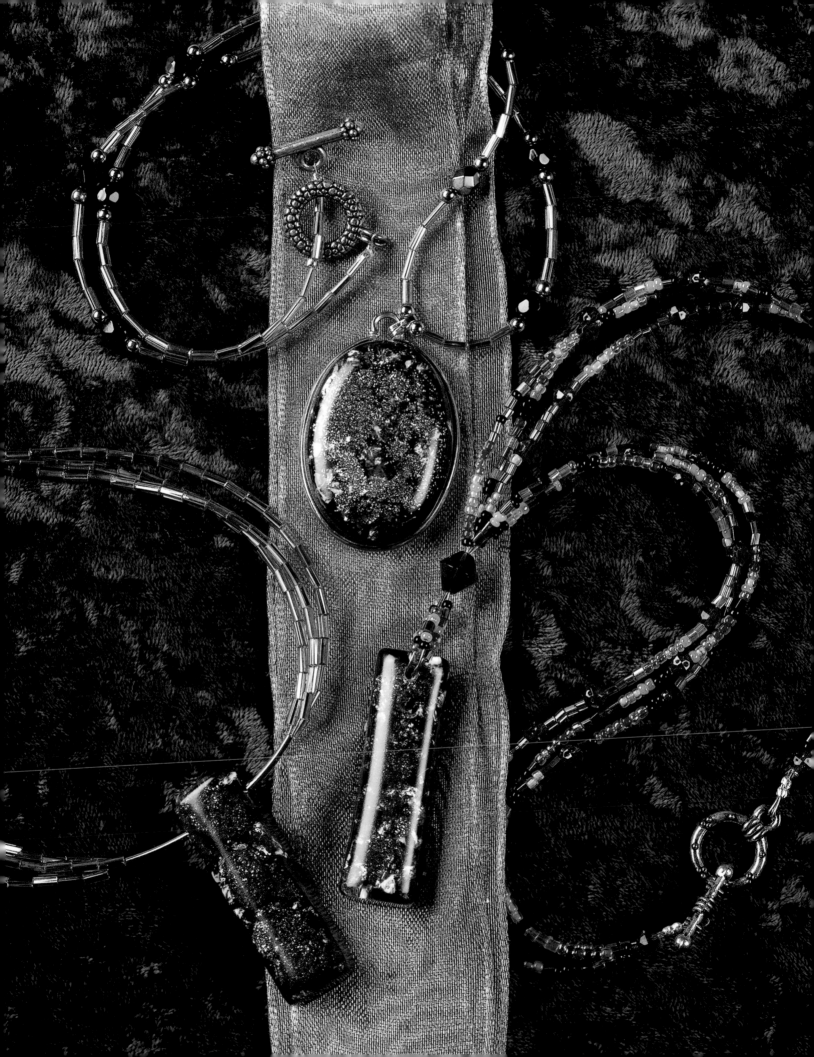

Faux Dichroic Bracelets

Both dichroic bracelets were created using the same techniques, but the cast pieces are different shapes.

supplies

Two-part epoxy casting resin

Jewelry mold with hexagonal cavities and trapezoid-shaped cavities

Mold release

Dichroic additives – Black colorant, iridescent flakes, colored glitter

Beads – Black iridescent E beads, 6 mm gold spacer beads

Clear elastic beading cord

Drill and 1/8" drill bit

Equipment from list of Basic Supplies. (See page 36.)

instructions

Make the Castings:

See the instructions for "Making Faux Gems."

1. Mix the resin with the dichroic additives and pour into the prepared hexagonal and trapezoid-shaped cavities in the mold. Let cure.
2. Release the pieces from the mold. Sand and polish the edges.
3. Using the photo as a guide, mark and drill two holes in the sides of each cast piece. Polish inside each drilled hole.

Assemble the Bracelets:

4. Thread the cast pieces on the beading cord, placing beads between each piece as shown in the photo.
5. Tie the ends of the cord in square knots and add a drop of mixed resin to each knot to secure. Let fully cure before using. ❏

Shell Necklace

Here's an example of how casting allows you to change the colors of nature. I used a real clamshell to make a latex mold to cast the pendant for this necklace. See "Making a Rubber Mold" in the Techniques section for mold-making instructions.

supplies

Two-part epoxy casting resin

Latex mold made from a small shell

Mold release

Transparent colorants – Blue, green

Beads – Green, blue, and silver metallic seed beads; mixed blue seed beads; iridescent fish beads; freshwater pearls

2 yds. silver beading cable

1 silver toggle clasp

2 silver crimping beads and crimping tool

Drill and 1/8" drill bit

Wire cutters

Equipment from list of Basic Supplies. (See page 36.)

instructions

1. Mix the resin with green and blue transparent colorants to make an aquamarine hue. Pour into the latex mold. Let cure.
2. Release from the mold. Sand and polish the edges.
3. Using a 1/8" drill bit, drill a hole across the top of the cast piece. Polish inside the hole.

Assemble the Necklace:

4. Cut the beading cable into three 24" lengths. Thread the cable pieces through the drilled hole and add 9" of beads on each side, using the photo as a guide, to create a princess-length necklace.
5. Attach the silver toggle clasp by running the beading cables on one side through one side of the clasp and back through a crimp bead. Crimp the bead to secure. Thread the remaining cable through the beads near the ends on that side and trim the excess cable. Repeat on the other side. ❑

Marbled Granite Knobs

Two different colors of granite powder are mixed with resin and poured together to create the marbled look. I used black and gray granite powders, but with the different colors of granite powder available, it's possible to choose colors to fit any color scheme.

supplies

Two-part epoxy casting resin

Square knob molds

Mold release

Granite powders – Black, gray

Silver knob hardware

Silver brads

Masking tape

Wire cutters

Equipment from list of Basic Supplies. (See page 36.)

instructions

1. Measure and mix the casting resin following the step by step instructions. Divide the mixed resin into two mixing cups.
2. To one cup, add black granite powder. To the other, add gray granite powder. Mix the granite powders and resin together well.
3. Pour the gray granite resin into the black granite resin and mix once gently to swirl the colors together.
4. Pour the resin into prepared molds to a depth of only 1/4". Let cure.
5. Release from the molds. Sand and polish the edges.
6. Using wire cutters, cut off the tops off the brads to make the silver accents.
7. Mix a small amount of epoxy resin and use to attach the silver accents and the knob hardware. Use masking tape to secure the pieces in place until the resin cures to prevent them from sliding. ❏

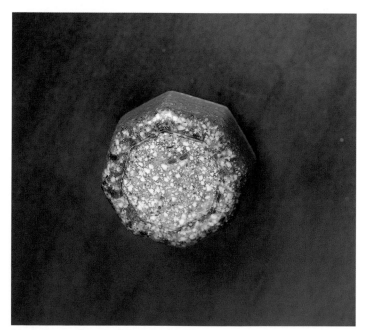

Variation using a different mold.

Marbled Granite Coasters

You could use this technique to make faux turquoise coasters for a southwestern
look or use the fantasy glass recipe for a modern, glittery effect. You'll need
one mold for each coaster you plan to make if you want to pour
them all at one time.

supplies

Two-part epoxy casting resin

Square resin mold, 3" x 3" x 1-1/16"
   deep, 5 ounce capacity

Mold release

Granite powders – Black, gray

Self-adhesive cork dots (4 for each
   coaster)

Equipment from list of Basic Supplies.
   (See page 36.)

instructions

1. Mix the casting resin following the general measuring and mixing instructions. Divide the mixed resin into two mixing cups.
2. To one cup, add black granite powder. To the other, add gray granite powder. Mix the granite powders and resin together well.
3. Pour the gray granite resin into the black granite resin and mix once gently to swirl the colors together.
4. Pour the resin into prepared molds to a depth of only 1/4". Let cure.
5. Release from the molds. Sand and polish the edges.
6. Attach the cork dots to the bottoms of the coasters. ❑

"Jade" Coasters

These faux jade coasters have been etched with the Chinese characters for earth, wind, fire, and water. The etched areas were filled with casting resin mixed with metallic gold powder for a dramatic accent. They would be a great accessory for Asian or contemporary decor.

You'll need one mold for each coaster you plan to make if you want to pour them all at one time.

supplies

Two-part epoxy casting resin

Square resin mold, 3" x 3" x 1-1/16" deep, 5 ounce capacity

Mold release

Additives for faux jade – Green and amber colorants, black polymer clay bits

Gold metallic powder

Chinese characters pattern

White transfer paper and stylus

Rotary tool with engraving bit

Self-adhesive cork dots (4 for each coaster)

Equipment from list of Basic Supplies. (See page 36.)

instructions

Cast:

See the instructions for "Making Faux Gems."

1. Measure and mix the casting resin following the step by step instructions. Add the jade additives and pour into the prepared molds to a depth of only 1/4". Let cure.
2. Released from the molds. Sand and polish the edges.

Etch:

3. Transfer the patterns to the tops of the cast coasters with white transfer paper.
4. Using a rotary tool with an engraving bit, etch the outlines of the symbols, following the patterns. Etch inside each outlined shape to a shallow (slightly less than) 1/8" depth.
5. Mix a small batch (2 ounces) of resin. Add gold metallic powder and stir well.
6. Carefully fill each etched-out shape with gold-colored resin. Let cure, being careful not to move the coasters until they are completely cured.

Finish:

7. Attach cork dots to the bottom of each coaster. ❑

"Jade" Cabinet Knobs

An actual old Chinese coin adorns each "jade" pull. I found these at an online auction site – old coins are generally less expensive than reproduction coins and have remarkable patinas.

supplies

Two-part epoxy casting resin

Round knob molds

Mold release

Additives for faux jade – Green and amber colorants, black polymer clay bits

Gold knob hardware

Old Chinese coins, 1 per knob

Masking tape

Equipment from list of Basic Supplies. (See page 36.)

instructions

Cast:

See the instructions for "Making Faux Gems."

1. Measure and mix the casting resin following the step by step instructions. Stir in the jade additives and pour into the prepared molds. Let cure.
2. Release from the molds. Sand and polish the edges.

Finish:

3. Mix a small amount of epoxy resin and use to attach the coin accents and the knob hardware. Use masking tape to secure the pieces in place until the resin cures to prevent them from sliding. ❑

"Jade" Switchplate

Using a plaster mold for the master, I made a latex mold to cast this switchplate. You could also use a switchplate from the hardware store as a master – choose a plate about 1/4" thick so the mold will be deep enough for the casting. The casting's final layer should be opaque so the wires and unfinished part of the wall don't show through the transparent jade.

supplies

Two-part epoxy casting resin

Latex mold made with a switchplate master (See "Creating a Master" in the Techniques section.)

Mold release

Faux jade additives – Green and amber colorants, black polymer clay bits

Gold metallic powder

Rotary drill with 1/4" drill bit

Equipment from list of Basic Supplies. (See page 36.)

instructions

1. Measure and mix the casting resin according to the step by step instructions. Incorporate the jade additives and pour into the prepared mold, filling the mold almost to the top. Let cure.
2. Mix another batch of resin – enough to completely fill the mold. Add gold metallic powder, mix, and use to fill the mold. Let cure.
3. Release the casting from the mold. Sand and polish the edges.
4. Drill the holes for screws, using a purchased switchplate as a guide for placement. ❑

Collection Casting

In this technique, objects that form a collection are coated with epoxy casting resin.
The excess resin is poured off and the objects are placed in a mold or free formed.
The thin layer of epoxy resin acts as a glue, holding the pieces together to form
a strong cast mass.
In this section you'll see a variety of tabletop and garden accessories using pebbles,
sea glass, shells, and river rocks. Other objects, such as chunks of rough rocks,
buttons, or coins, also could be used.

basic supplies for collection casting

- **Two-part epoxy casting resin**
- **Objects to form castings** – Pebbles, sea glass, shells, river rocks, buttons, coins, marbles
- **Molds**, to shape the collections. IMPORTANT: Never use a bowl for food after using it as a mold for resin!
- **Mold release agent**, if you're using a mold (Choose an appropriate release agent for the type of mold.)
- **Equipment – You will need the following for each project:**

Mixing cups – disposable graduated plastic cups

Wooden stir stick, for mixing

Plastic mesh, to act as a strainer for excess resin. You can find inexpensive plastic needlework mesh at crafts and sewing centers.

Disposable container, such as a plastic bowl, for holding the excess resin as the collection drains

Latex gloves, to protect your hands

Freezer paper, to protect your work surface

Two bowls. The one on the left is made with white flatback marbles.
The one on the right is made with clear round marbles.

collection casting, step by step

These instructions, for making a bowl from clear glass flat-back marbles, show how the Collection Casting process is done.

1. Warm, Measure, and Mix.
Begin the process by following the steps for warming, measuring, and mixing the epoxy casting resin. See "Epoxy Resin Casting, Step by Step – The Two-Cup Method."

2. Add the Objects.
In this case, the objects are clear marbles.
Add the objects to the mixed resin. Stir to make sure all the pieces are well coated with resin.

3. Drain Off Excess Resin.
Cut a piece of plastic mesh larger than the top of the container you are using for draining. Place the mesh over the container. Place the resin-coated objects on the plastic mesh. (Photo 1) The excess resin will drain into the container. Leave the objects to drain for about 10 minutes. Move them around to be sure all the excess resin has a chance to drip off before the resin starts to set up.

4. Position the Objects in the Mold.
Wearing latex gloves, pick up the sticky resin-covered objects and place them in the mold. Here, I'm placing inside a plastic bowl that I am using as a mold, lining the bottom and the sides with the marbles. (Photo 2)

5. Release Bubbles.
Use a hair dryer to remove any bubbles on the resin.

6. Allow to Harden.
Let the cast piece cure at least 12 hours before removing from the mold.

7. Release from the Mold and Cure.
Release the casting from the mold. Allow to cure fully (24 hours).

8. Finish.
Sand away drips on the outside of the casting, using a rotary tool with fine sandpaper. Finish the piece by polishing the sanded areas with carnauba polish.

Photo 1 – Draining the excess resin from the glass marbles.

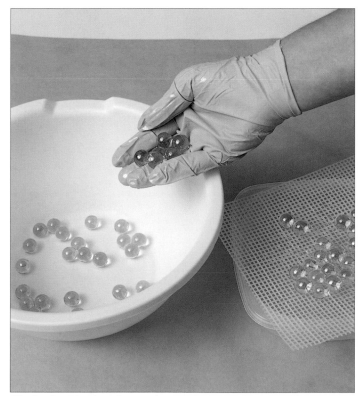

Photo 2 – Placing the resin-coated glass marbles in the plastic bowl mold.

Pebble Collection

These pieces are made of small polished river pebbles – the kind you can buy in the floral departments of craft and home decor stores. The pebbles I used were a pale ochre color, but you can substitute any color to coordinate with your furnishings.

PEBBLE SOAP DISH

Coated pebbles are stacked in a mold to make this soap dish. I used dome knob castings to make the feet and glued them to the bottom. To clean the soap dish, simply hold under running warm water and wipe with a soft cloth.

supplies

Two-part epoxy casting resin

Rectangular resin mold, 3" x 6" x 1-1/16" deep, 9 ounce capacity

Dome knob mold

Mold release

Pale ochre pebbles, 1 to 1-1/2" in diameter

Small ochre pebbles, 1/4 to 1/2" diameter

Equipment from list of Basic Supplies. (See page 56.)

instructions
Make the Soap Dish:
1. Warm, measure, and mix the epoxy casting resin. See "Epoxy Resin Casting, Step by Step."
2. Add the large pebbles to the mixed resin. Drain. See "Collection Casting, Step by Step."
3. Place the large pebbles in the prepared rectangular mold. Let cure.
4. Release from the mold.

Add the Feet:
5. Prepare four cavities of the dome knob mold.
6. Warm, measure, and mix the epoxy casting resin.
7. Place a few small pebbles in each mold cavity. Fill the mold cavities with the clear mixed resin. Let cure.
8. Release from the mold. Glue in place on the bottom of the soap dish, using a newly mixed batch of resin. Let cure completely before using. ❑

PEBBLE CANDLEHOLDER

This pebble candle base was done in three steps. The glass candleholders are permanently attached to the base.

supplies

Two-part epoxy casting resin

Dome knob mold

Ochre colored pebbles, 1/4 to 1/2" diameter

2 glass votive holders

1 glass tea light holder

Equipment from list of Basic Supplies. (See page 56.)

instructions
Make the Pebbles Base:
1. Warm, measure, and mix the epoxy casting resin. See "Epoxy Resin Casting, Step by Step."
2. Add about a third of the pebbles to the mixed resin and mix to coat. Drain. See "Collection Casting, Step by Step."
3. Arrange the pebbles on freezer paper in an 8" diameter circle. Let cure.
4. Mix another batch of resin, add another third of the pebbles, mix to coat, and drain.
5. Arrange in a layer over the first layer of pebbles. Let cure.
6. Arrange the glass candleholders on the cured pebble mat, using pebbles to level them as needed.
7. Mix another batch of resin, add more pebbles, and drain.
8. Arrange the resin-coated pebbles around the glass candleholders to secure. Let cure.
9. Sand away any excess resin from the edge of the pebble base. Polish the sanded areas.

Feet:
10. Prepare four cavities of the dome knob mold.
11. Warm, measure, and mix the epoxy casting resin.
12. Place a few pebbles in each mold cavity. Fill the mold cavities with the clear mixed resin. Let cure.
13. Release from the mold. Glue in place on the bottom of the pebble base, using a newly mixed batch of resin. Let cure completely before using. ❑

Continued on page 60

Pebble Collection, continued

PEBBLE BOWL

I used a plastic bowl as a mold; you can create higher sides by piling the resin-covered pebbles up along the sides of the mold. Never use a bowl for food after using it as a mold for resin!

supplies

Two-part epoxy casting resin

Dome knob mold

Bowl mold (I used a small, inexpensive, very flexible plastic bowl.)

Mold release (paste wax)

Ochre pebbles, 1/4 to 1/2" diameter

Equipment from list of Basic Supplies. (See page 56.)

instructions

1. Wipe a thin layer of paste wax on the inside of the plastic bowl. TIP: Test the flexibility of your bowl to make sure the pebbles will release.
2. Warm, measure, and mix the epoxy casting resin. See "Epoxy Resin Casting, Step by Step."
3. Add the pebbles to the mixed resin. Drain. See "Collection Casting, Step by Step."
4. Arrange them on the bottom and up the sides of the bowl mold. Let cure.
5. Release from the mold. Sand away any excess resin and polish the sanded areas.

Feet:

6. Prepare four cavities of the dome knob mold.
7. Warm, measure, and mix the epoxy casting resin.
8. Place a few pebbles in each mold cavity. Fill the mold cavities with the clear mixed resin. Let cure.
9. Release from the mold. Glue in place on the bottom of the bowl, using a newly mixed batch of resin. Let cure completely before using. ❏

PEBBLE KNOBS

supplies

Two-part epoxy casting resin

Pale ochre pebbles, 1" to 1-1/2" diameter, one per knob

Ochre pebbles, 1/4" to 1/2" diameter, two or three per knob

Gold knob hardware

Masking tape

Equipment from list of Basic Supplies. (See page 56.)

instructions

1. Warm, measure, and mix the epoxy casting resin. See "Epoxy Resin Casting, Step by Step."
2. Add all the pebbles to the mixed resin. Stir to coat. Drain. See "Collection Casting, Step by Step."
3. Place the pebbles on freezer paper, arranging a few small pebbles on and beside a large pebble. Let cure completely.
4. Sand sharp resin from the edges and polish.
5. Mix a small amount of epoxy resin and use as a glue to attach the knob hardware. Secure the pebble clusters with masking tape to prevent them from sliding until they are cured. ❏

PEBBLE TILES

These accent tiles look especially nice when used with tumbled marble tiles – a single row makes a dramatic impact, and they are practical as well. The stones are permanently attached and won't fall off, even in a high traffic area. Clean them by washing with water or dusting with a soft, clean bristle brush.

supplies

Two-part epoxy casting resin

Pale ochre pebbles, 1/4 to 1/2" diameter. You'll need about 1/4 cup of pebbles for each 4" square tile.

4" square ceramic tiles

Small plastic cups

Equipment from list of Basic Supplies. (See page 56.)

instructions

1. Raise the tiles off your freezer paper covered work surface by placing them on small plastic cups.
2. Warm, measure, and mix the epoxy casting resin. See "Epoxy Resin Casting, Step by Step."
3. Add the pebbles to the mixed resin. Drain. See "Collection Casting, Step by Step."
4. Arrange the drained pebbles on the tiles, making sure they do not extend beyond the edges of the tiles. Do not worry if excess resin flows over the sides of the tiles.
5. Let the resin cure completely. Sand off any resin drips from the sides or bottoms of the tiles.

To attach the tiles to a wall: Use mastic intended for tile. Let dry. Use sand-less grout, applying the grout between the tiles. Try not to get grout on the tops of the pebble tiles. If you do, wash off the grout immediately. ❑

61

Seashell Collection

Shells are a natural and beautiful material to use for casting. The finished pieces look
wonderful in beach and natural-themed environments and give the relaxed feeling of a
tropical holiday.

SEASHELL CANDLEHOLDER

supplies

Two-part epoxy casting resin

Mold – I used a clean wax-coated paper carton, cut to 4"
high

Small to medium sized seashells

Glass tea light holder

Equipment from list of Basic Supplies. (See page 56.)

instructions

1. Warm, measure, and mix the epoxy casting resin. See "Epoxy
   Resin Casting, Step by Step."
2. Add all the pebbles to the mixed resin. Stir to coat. Drain. See
   "Collection Casting, Step by Step."
3. Arrange the shells in the carton to a height of 3". Place the glass
   tea light on top of the shells and arrange more shells around it
   to hold it in place. Let cure.
4. Peel away the paper carton mold. If needed, sand away excess
   resin from the sides of the piece and polish the sanded areas. ❑

SEASHELL COASTERS

I used the traditional casting technique to make these coasters to ensure a level surface
for placing glasses and cups. The granite powder added to the second pouring
has the look of beach sand.

supplies

Two-part epoxy casting resin

Square resin molds, 3" x 3" x 1-1/16" deep, 5 ounce capacity

Mold release

Small seashells

Dried starfish, 1 for each coaster

Sand colored granite powder

Self-adhesive cork dots

Equipment from list of Basic Supplies. (See page 56.)

instructions

1. Prepare the molds.
2. Warm, measure, and mix the epoxy casting resin. See "Epoxy
   Resin Casting, Step by Step." Pour into the prepared molds to
   a depth of only 1/4".
3. Arrange the shells and starfish in the molds, right sides down.
   Let cure.
4. Mix a new batch of the resin. Stir in the granite powder. Pour
   into the molds over the cured shell layer to a depth of 1/4". Let
   cure.
5. Release from the molds. Sand and polish the edges.
6. Attach cork dots to the bottoms of the coasters. ❑

Seashell Collection, continued

SEASHELL KNOBS
These cast knobs bring the seashore to cabinet doors and drawers.

supplies

Two-part epoxy casting resin

Dome knob molds

Mold release

Small seashells

Sand colored granite powder

Gold knob hardware

Masking tape

Equipment from list of Basic Supplies.
  (See page 56.)

instructions

1. Prepare the mold cavities.
2. Warm, measure, and mix the epoxy casting resin. See "Epoxy Resin Casting, Step by Step." Pour into the prepared molds to a depth of only 1/4".
3. Arrange the shells in the mold cavities, right sides down. Let cure.
4. Mix a new batch of the resin. Stir in the granite powder. Pour into the mold cavities over the cured shell layer and fill to the top of each mold cavity. Let cure.
5. Release from the molds. Sand and polish the edges.
6. Mix a small amount of epoxy resin. Use it to attach the knob hardware. Secure the castings with masking tape to prevent them from sliding until they are cured. ❏

SEASHELL BOWL

Any glass vessel can be enhanced with resin-covered shells. They will permanently adhere to the glass surface, are waterproof, and can be cleaned with water. A bowl with sloping sides is more of a challenge than a flat surface. TIP: Let the resin on the shells get very sticky before arranging.

supplies

Two-part epoxy casting resin

Seashells, small to large sizes

Dried starfish

Coral sand

Fish netting (I used the dark net that the shells were sold in.)

Low glass bowl with shallow sides

Equipment from list of Basic Supplies. (See page 56.)

instructions

1. Place the bowl upside down on a freezer paper covered surface.
2. Warm, measure, and mix the epoxy casting resin. See "Epoxy Resin Casting, Step by Step"
3. Add the shells to the mixed resin, reserving a few shells to use on the rim of the bowl later. Stir to coat. Drain. See "Collection Casting, Step by Step."
4. Arrange the netting on the sides of bowl. (The netting will help hold the shells in place.)
5. Arrange the shells over the netting.
6. Coat the coral sand with resin and add to the arrangement. Don't worry if excess resin pools at the bowl's edge. Let cure.
7. Remove the bowl from the freezer paper and set upright. Sand away any resin drips from the rim of the bowl. Polish the sanded areas.
8. Mix a new batch of resin and add the reserved shells. Stir to coat with resin.
9. Arrange the shells on the lip of the bowl. The previous layer of resin-coated shells will have formed a level ridge around the rim. Place the shells on this rim. Wipe off any resin that drips inside the bowl with a clean, dry paper towel. ❑

SEASHELL VASE WITH FAUX CORAL

Resin-covered objects can also be placed on glass vases.
They will permanently adhere to the glass surface, are
waterproof, and can be cleaned with water.

supplies

For the vase:

Two-part epoxy casting resin

Seashells, small to large sizes

Dried starfish

Coral sand

Fish netting (I used the dark net that the shells were sold in.)

Rectangular glass vase

Small plastic cups

Equipment from list of Basic Supplies. (See page 56.)

For the faux coral:

Dried tree or shrub branches

Acrylic craft paint – Orange coral

High gloss acrylic spray sealer

Paint brush

instructions

Decorate the Vase:

1. Place the vase on its back and raise it off the freezer paper covered surface with small plastic cups.
2. Warm, measure, and mix the epoxy casting resin. See "Epoxy Resin Casting, Step by Step."
3. Add the shells to the mixed resin. Stir to coat. Drain. See "Collection Casting, Step by Step."
4. Arrange the netting on the front of the vase. (The netting will help hold the shells in place.)
5. Arrange the shells over the netting.
6. Coat the coral sand with resin and add to the arrangement. Don't worry if excess resin drips down the sides of the vase. Let cure.
7. Sand away any drips of resin on the back or bottom of the vase and polish the sanded areas.

Make the Faux Coral:

8. Trim the branches so they resemble coral.
9. Basecoat with orange coral acrylic paint to cover completely. (Two or three coats should do it.) Let dry between coats.
10. When the last coat of paint is completely dry, spray the branches with high gloss acrylic spray. Let dry.
11. Arrange in the vase with additional shells and coral sand. ❏

Sea Glass Collection

The Collection Casting technique provides a variety of opportunities for enjoying the colors of sea glass – when coated with epoxy resin, the glass shines and sparkles. You can collect sea glass at the beach or buy bags of inexpensive tumbled glass ("sea glass") in the floral and mosaic departments of crafts shops.

SEA GLASS TILES

Inexpensive plain white ceramic tiles provide the base for
these sea glass decorated tiles. You only need a few for a
dramatic impact on a tiled wall.

supplies

Two-part epoxy casting resin

Sea glass, 1" to 1-1/2" pieces

White ceramic tiles, 4" square

Small plastic cups

Equipment from list of Basic Supplies.
  (See page 56.)

instructions

1. Elevate the tiles above your freezer
   paper covered surface with small plastic
   cups.
2. Warm, measure, and mix the epoxy
   casting resin. See "Epoxy Resin Casting,
   Step by Step."
3. Add the shells to the mixed resin. Stir to
   coat. Drain. See "Collection Casting,
   Step by Step."
4. Arrange the glass pieces on the tiles,
   making sure the glass pieces don't
   extend beyond the edges of the tiles. Do
   not worry if excess resin flows over the
   sides. Let the resin cure completely.
5. Sand off resin drips from the backs of
   the tiles.

To attach the tiles to a wall: Use mastic
intended for tile. Let dry. Use sand-less
grout, applying the grout between the tiles.
Try not to get grout on the tops of the glass
tiles. If you do, wash off the grout immediately. ❑

Sea Glass Collection, continued

SEA GLASS CANDLEHOLDER

This is a simple way to decorate a glass votive holder. The
sea glass is piled around the holder and left to cure.

supplies

Two-part epoxy casting resin

Sea glass, 1 to 1-1/2" pieces

Glass votive holder

Equipment from list of Basic Supplies. (See page 56.)

instructions

1. Warm, measure, and mix the epoxy casting resin. See "Epoxy Resin Casting, Step by Step."
2. Add the sea glass to the mixed resin. Stir to coat. Drain. See "Collection Casting, Step by Step."
3. Place the candleholder on a piece of freezer paper. Arrange the drained sea glass pieces around the candleholder, placing larger glass pieces around the base and smaller, flatter glass pieces up the sides. Let cure.
4. Sand away any excess resin from the edges. Polish the sanded areas. ❏

SEA GLASS SOAP DISH

This footless soap dish looks beautiful with transparent soap.
Wash the soap dish by running under warm water and wiping
with a soft cloth.

supplies

Two-part epoxy casting resin

Rectangular resin mold, 3" x 6" x 1-1/16" deep, 9 ounce capacity

Mold release

Sea glass, 1" to 1-1/2" pieces

Equipment from list of Basic Supplies. (See page 56.)

instructions

1. Warm, measure, and mix the epoxy casting resin. See "Epoxy Resin Casting, Step by Step."
2. Add the sea glass to the mixed resin. Stir to coat. Drain. See "Collection Casting, Step by Step."
3. Place the glass pieces in the prepared rectangular mold. Let cure.
4. Release from the mold. If necessary, sand away excess resin. Polish the sanded areas. ❏

Sea Glass Collection, continued

SEA GLASS NIGHTLIGHT

You can find small plastic lights at craft stores. With the
addition of sea glass, they offer a sparkling guiding
light at night.

supplies

Two-part epoxy casting resin

Rectangular resin mold, 2" x 2 1/2" x
   1-1/16" deep, 3 ounce capacity

Mold release

Sea glass, 1" to 1-1/2" pieces

White plastic nightlight

Equipment from list of Basic Supplies.
   (See page 56.)

instructions

1. Warm, measure, and mix the epoxy
   casting resin. See "Epoxy Resin Casting,
   Step by Step."
2. Add the sea glass to the mixed resin.
   Stir to coat. Drain. See "Collection
   Casting, Step by Step."
3. Place the glass pieces in the prepared
   rectangular mold. Arrange the nightlight in the sea glass, making sure it is
   flush with the top of the mold. Let cure.
4. Release from the mold. If necessary,
   sand away excess resin. Polish the sanded areas. ❏

SEASHELL CABINET KNOBS

I used real shells to make the molds for these cast cabinet knobs.
The green and blue colorants coordinate beautifully with the colors
of sea glass, and a light coat of gloss spray provides shine.
TIP: When making latex molds for custom knobs, make at least
four. It takes about the same amount of time to make multiple molds
as it does to make one, and having multiple molds makes the casting
a much quicker job.

supplies

Two-part epoxy casting resin

Custom latex shell molds (See "Making a Rubber Mold.")

Mold release

Transparent colorants – Green, blue

Silver knob hardware

Small plastic cups

Masking tape

Equipment from list of Basic Supplies. (See page 36.)

instructions

1. Condition the molds with mold release and let dry. See "Rubber Mold, Step by Step."
2. Place the molds in small plastic cups to hold them level while you pour.
3. Warm, measure, and mix the epoxy casting resin. See "Epoxy Resin Casting, Step by Step." Add green and blue colorants to make a transparent aquamarine hue.
4. Pour the colored resin into the molds. Let cure.
5. Release from the molds. If needed, sand the edges of the cast shells and polish the sanded areas.
6. Spray the cast shells with clear gloss spray. Let dry.
7. Mix a small amount of the epoxy resin and use to attach the knob hardware. Secure the pieces with masking tape while they cure to prevent them from sliding. ❑

Cast Mat Frames

This new technique uses picture frames as molds for casting decorative mats. Layers of resin are poured between the frames, gradually building up layers to fill the space. Use this technique to create personalized frames for unique gifts. Many types of objects can be embedded in the clear resin layers to create one-of-a-kind pieces, but *never* encase anything rare or one-of-a-kind in the resin. Objects embedded in the resin cannot be removed.

supplies for cast mat frames

- **Two-part epoxy casting resin**
- **Objects for embedding** – Many objects can be used. For example, I have tried plastic fruit, silk leaves and flowers, coins, shells, metal memorabilia.
- **Frames** – 2 for each project, a large frame and a smaller frame. They do not need to match, or even be made of the same material; both wooden and metal frames will work. I used very inexpensive frames for my projects.
- **Transparent colorants,** for tinted mats
- **Equipment – You will need the following for each project:**
  Double-sided tape
  Mixing cups – disposable graduated plastic cups
  Wooden stir stick, for mixing
  Disposable glue brush, *Optional* for leveling the resin after pouring
  Latex gloves, to protect your hands
  Freezer paper, to protect your working surface and serve as the bottom of the mold. The cast resin mats will separate nicely with a clear, clean finish. You can also use wax paper, but most projects need a wider base, and wax paper gives a cloudy, matte finish.
  Hair dryer, for removing bubbles in the resin

cast mat frames, step by step

The Military Hat Badges Frame is used as an example to show how the Cast Mat Frames process is done.

1. Prepare the Frames.
Remove the glass and backing from the frames. Reserve the glass and backing from the center frame. (You don't need the glass or backing from the larger frame for this project.) Apply double-stick tape to the back edges of both frames. Don't leave any gaps. If the frame material is narrow (narrower than the tape), leave excess tape on the outside of the larger frame and on the inside of the smaller frame.

2. Place on Work Surface.
Place freezer paper, shiny side up, on a smooth, hard, level work surface. Place the larger frame on the work surface, pressing it against the surface so the tape is firmly holding the frame to the freezer paper with no gaps. Position the smaller frame inside the larger frame, placing it towards the top of the inside space, making sure everything is straight. Press this frame down securely as well. Fold up all the edges of the freezer paper 1/2" in case the resin leaks out.

3. Warm, Measure, and Mix the Resin.
Follow the steps for warming, measuring, and mixing the epoxy casting resin. See "Epoxy Resin Casting, Step by Step – The Two-Cup Method." Mix no more than 6 ounces at a time.

4. Pour the First Layer.
Pour the first layer into the space between the frames. It will level out and fill the entire space. If needed, use a disposable glue brush to make sure the entire surface is covered. The resin should not leak under the frames, but if it does, don't worry – it is easy to trim off after it sets.

5. Add Objects and Let Set.
Remove any bubbles on the surface with a hair dryer on low speed. At this point, add your chosen objects to the resin, arranging them where you want them in the finished piece. (You can add more objects in each layer if you wish a dimensional look.) Let set until firm.

6. Pour the Second (and Succeeding) Layer(s).
When the first layer of resin is firm, you can pour the second layer. (Photo) To pour additional layers, repeat the warming, measuring, mixing steps. Pour as many 6-ounce layers as needed to fill the space between the frames and let cure until firm between pourings. In each layer, you can add additional objects. *Option:* You can also tint the resin for a colored transparent mat.

7. Allow to Cure.
When you have poured all the layers, let the frame cure completely – at least 48 hours.

8. Finish.
Peel off the freezer paper and remove the tape from the back of the frame. If needed, trim away any resin that leaked under the frame. (TIP: If you have trouble removing the tape, apply some ordinary cellophane tape to cover the sticky surface.) Add a sawtooth hanger to the top of the back of the large frame. Replace the glass, add a photograph or print, and replace the backing on the small frame.

MILITARY HAT BADGE COLLECTION FRAME
Instructions begin on page 76.

MILITARY HAT BADGE COLLECTION FRAME
Pictured on page 75.

The photograph in the small frame inspired this design.
A collection of military hat badges was embedded into the resin
mat. You can use this idea to feature sports medals or awards, but
remember the placement of the badges or medals is permanent,
and they cannot be removed.

supplies

Two-part epoxy casting resin

Oak frame, 4" x 6"

Oak frame, 8-1/2" x 11"

Metal hat badges

Equipment from list of Basic Supplies. (See page 74.)

instructions

*Three layers of resin, 4 ounces each, were poured into the space
between the frames to fill the space.*

1. Prepare the badges by removing any metal pieces that protrude on the back so they will lay flat on the surface.
2. Following the step-by-step instructions for Cast Mat Frames at the beginning of this section, prepare the frames, apply the double-stick tape, position the frames on the freezer-paper covered work surface, and warm, measure, and mix 4 ounces of resin.
3. Pour the first 4 ounces of resin. Let cure until firm.
4. Arrange the badges in the space between the frames, using the project photo as a guide.
5. Measure and mix another 4 ounces of resin. Pour. Let cure until firm.
6. Measure and mix another 4 ounces of resin. Pour. Let cure 48 hours.
7. Place a print or photograph in the small frame. ❑

TUSCAN OLIVE GARDEN FRAME

This cast mat is perfect for a room with Italian-inspired decor.

supplies

Two-part epoxy casting resin

Blue colorant

Dark wooden frame, 5" x 7"

Dark wooden frame, 11" x 14"

Objects to embed – Plastic olives and silk leaves

Equipment from list of Basic Supplies. (See page 74.)

instructions

*Three layers of resin, 6 ounces each, were poured into the space
between the frames to fill the space.*

1. Following the step-by-step instructions for Cast Mat Frames at the beginning of this section, prepare the frames, apply the double-stick tape, position the frames on the freezer-paper covered work surface, and warm, measure, and mix 6 ounces of resin.
2. Divide the first resin batch into two mixing cups. Tint one cup with a little blue colorant. Pour the tinted resin at the top and around the center frame. Pour the clear resin at the bottom of the frame. Use a stir stick to blend the resins together where they meet. Let cure until firm.
3. Place the olives and leaves on the resin. Measure and mix another 6 ounces of clear resin. Pour. Let cure until firm.
4. Mix 6 ounces of clear resin for the final layer. Pour around, but not over, the plastic olives. Let cure 48 hours.
5. Place a print or photograph in the small frame. ❑

SEASHELL FRAME

This seashell frame is a nice addition to other Seashell Collection cast pieces.

supplies

Two-part epoxy casting resin

Matte silver metal frame, 4" x 6"

Matte silver metal frame, 8-1/2 " x 11"

Objects to embed – Shells, fish netting, coral sand, mini dried starfish

Equipment from list of Basic Supplies. (See page 74.)

instructions

Three layers of resin, 6 ounces each, were poured into the space between the frames to fill the space.

1. Following the step-by-step instructions for Cast Mat Frames at the beginning of this section, prepare the frames, apply the double-stick tape, position the frames on the freezer-paper covered work surface, and warm, measure, and mix 6 ounces of resin.

2. Pour the resin in the space between the frames. Let cure until firm.

3. Using the photo as a guide, place netting, shells, and starfish on the resin around the bottom and slightly up the sides of the inner space.

4. Measure and mix another 6 ounces of clear resin. Add a few small shells and some coral sand. Mix. Pour. Let cure until firm.

5. Mix 6 ounces of clear resin for the final layer. Pour over the shells. Let cure 48 hours.

6. Place a print or photograph in the small frame. ❏

ASIAN ORCHID FRAME

This frame was designed for a room with Asian-themed decor.
It would coordinate nicely with the cast "jade" projects.

supplies

Two-part epoxy casting resin

Dark wooden frame with gold highlights, 4" x 6"

Dark wooden frame with gold highlights, 11" x 14"

Objects to embed – Silk orchids, silk ferns, small pebbles, plastic lizard

Equipment from list of Basic Supplies. (See page 74.)

instructions

Three layers of resin, 6 ounces each, were poured into the area between the frames to fill the space.

1. Following the step-by-step instructions for Cast Mat Frames at the beginning of this section, prepare the frames, apply the double-stick tape, position the frames on the freezer-paper covered work surface, and warm, measure, and mix 6 ounces of resin.

2. Pour the resin in the space between the frames. Let cure until firm.

3. Using the photo as a guide, arrange the pebbles and plastic lizard around the bottom of the inner frame.

4. Measure and mix another 6 ounces of clear resin. Pour. Allow to cure until firm.

5. Arrange the orchids and ferns on the side of the frame.

6. Mix 6 ounces of clear resin for the final layer. Pour over the orchids and ferns. Let cure 48 hours.

7. Place a print or photograph in the small frame. ❏

VINTAGE PENNY FRAME

A vintage photograph is the perfect complement to this copper penny mat. Another idea would be a vacation photograph of travels to another country – then use the coins from that country.

supplies

Two-part epoxy casting resin

Amber colorant

Wooden frame, 5" x 7"

Wooden frame, 8-1/2" x 11"

Penny coins

Equipment from list of Basic Supplies. (See page 74.)

instructions

Three layers of resin, 4 ounces each, were poured into the area between the frames to fill the space.

1. Following the step-by-step instructions for Cast Mat Frames at the beginning of this section, prepare the frames, apply the double-stick tape, position the frames on the freezer-paper covered work surface, and warm, measure, and mix 4 ounces of resin. Add amber colorant. Mix.

2. Arrange one-third of the pennies around the inner frame. Pour the resin in the space between the frames. Let cure until firm.

3. Mix 4 ounces clear resin. Arrange another third of the pennies around the inner frame. Pour. Let cure until firm.

4. Arrange the remaining pennies on the firm resin. Mix another four ounces of clear resin. Pour to cover all the coins. Let cure 48 hours.

5. Place a print or photograph in the small frame. ❏

DAISY PHOTO FRAME

This contemporary mat is decorated with dried,
pressed daisies and laser cut lettering designed as a scrapbooking embellishment.

supplies

Two-part epoxy casting resin

Silver frame, 5-1/2" square

Silver frame, 11-1/2" x 14-1/2"

Dried pressed daisies

Laser cut words, 1" high

White glue

Glue brush

Equipment from list of Basic Supplies.
  (See page 74.)

instructions

*Three layers of resin, 6 ounces each, were
poured into the area between the frames
to fill the space.*

1. Brush two coats of white glue over the
   letters to seal them. Let dry between
   coats, and let the last coat dry completely.

2. Following the step-by-step instructions
   for Cast Mat Frames at the beginning of
   this section, prepare the frames, apply
   the double-stick tape, position the
   frames on the freezer-paper covered
   work surface, and warm, measure, and
   mix 6 ounces of resin.

3. Pour. Let cure until firm.

4. Arrange the words on the resin, using
   the photo as a guide.

5. Mix 6 ounces of clear resin. Pour. Let
   cure until firm.

6. Arrange the daisies in the space
   between the frames, using the photo as
   a guide.

7. Mix 6 ounces of clear resin. Pour. Let
   cure 48 hours.

8. Place a print or photograph in the small
   frame. ❑

Plaster Casting

techniques & projects

Gypsum (hydrated calcium sulfate), a common natural mineral, is a sedimentary rock that was formed by evaporating sea water. Gypsum that is treated with heat and ground to a fine powder forms plaster. The large gypsum deposit at Montmartre in Paris is the source of the original plaster of Paris – a basic, easily found casting plaster.

Usually white in color and very soft, gypsum is one of the most widely used minerals in the world. When re-hydrated with water, it reacts chemically to form a rigid, strong crystal. We use gypsum to make chalk, drywall sheets, and surgical casts; it is also mixed with soy milk to firm up tofu.

In casting, plaster is used to quickly create paintable castings for use in home decor. With the easy painting recipes in this section, you can create the look of metals, terra cotta, and antiques.

Casting the Piece

molds

Almost any slightly flexible plastic mold can be used for plaster castings. Plastic molds manufactured for candy, soap, and plaster are easy to find in a wide range of designs. You can also make latex rubber molds for casting plaster.

Mold Preparation:

1. Clean the mold with a dry brush to remove dust and plaster bits from previous castings.
2. Mark the top of the mold with a black marker to indicate the top. (This comes in handy when you are adding a hanger after pouring and don't remember which side is the top.)
3. Spray the mold with a surfactant to reduce the surface tension and help prevent air bubbles.

Mold Support:

Whether you need a backup shell or something to support the mold depends on the size, material, weight, and shape of the mold.

If the mold will warp if wet plaster is poured in, you need a backup shell. Latex molds always need a backup shell or a support to hold the flange while pouring the plaster.

Leveling the mold is also important. Plastic molds that are not self-leveling or molds that tip when plaster is poured into a cavity need to be placed in a container of sand to prevent the mold from tipping and to keep it level.

plaster casting, basic supplies

- **Casting Plaster** – Many different types of casting plasters are available, including ones with additives such as glues, resins, and fibers to make the castings stronger. Look for these superior blends in crafts and art outlets.
- **Mold,** see chart in beginning of book to find the bests molds to use for this materials. There are a wide range of molds available made specifically for plaster casting
- **Surfactant,** to use as a mold release
- **Mold support,** such as a container with dry sand
- **Saw tooth hanger,** hardware to use for hanging the casting if it is a wallhanging piece

equipment for each project:

- **Water** to add to plaster
- **Flexible plastic bucket or bowl,** for mixing
- **Plaster blender,** which attaches to an electric drill, for blending
- **Electric drill,** to use with the plaster blender
- **Container,** for water
- **Strainer,** for sifting the plaster
- **Plaster knife,** or a sharp, non-serrated knife, for trimming
- **Sanding sponge** (a fine abrasive surface mounted on a soft sponge), for smoothing trimmed areas
- **Old towels,** for turning out the casting
- **Latex gloves,** to protect your hands
- **Wire rack,** for drying cast pieces

plaster casting supplies & equipment

Plaster Tools pictured: 1. Flexible plastic mixing bowl, 2. Plaster blender, 3. Container of sand to support a mold, 4. Mold (a latex mold with a backup mold, 5. Surfactant, 6. Casting plaster, 7. Old towels, 8. Sanding sponge, 9. Plaster knife, 10. Sawtooth hangers

plaster casting, step by step

Most plasters are mixed three parts plaster to two parts water by weight. Some harder casting plasters use a different ratio – two parts casting material to one part water. Generally, the more plaster used, the harder and stronger the casting. The instructions that follow present a basic plaster mixing method for obtaining the proper ratio without measuring the plaster and water.

1. Prepare the Mold(s).
Prepare the molds by applying a surfactant mold release. Make sure mold is level and that it is supported if needed.

2. Place the Water in the Mixing Bowl.
To determine the amount of water needed for your casting, fill the mold with water, and pour that amount of water in the mixing bowl. Do not fill the mixing bowl more than half full to ensure enough room for mixing. Use cold water – it will keep the plaster from setting up too quickly. TIP: Record the amount of water needed for each mold.

Option: You can add white glue or acrylic sealant that is manufactured as a plaster additive to the plaster mix to make the casting stronger. *If you use glue,* mix it with the water before adding the plaster, using 1 part glue to 10 parts water. *If you use an acrylic additive,* follow the manufacturer's instructions for mixing.

3. Add the Plaster.
Add plaster to the water by slowly sifting a small amount. (Photo 1) **Do not** add water to plaster – **always** add plaster to water. Continue adding plaster until a small mound forms above the water line in the center of the container. Stop when the plaster mound is about 1" above the water line. If you use too much plaster, the mix will be too thick and won't pour. If you use too little plaster, the casting will be brittle. Let the plaster absorb the water – **do not** mix now.

4. Mix the Plaster.
After the water is absorbed, mix the plaster and water. If you are mixing a large batch, use a plaster mixer on the end of an electric drill. For smaller batches, I wear latex gloves and mix with my hands – that way, I can feel the mixture and make sure I have the right consistency. Mix slowly to avoid trapping air in the mixture, and aim for a smooth mixture about the consistency of heavy cream. When you have finished mixing, tap the bowl a few times to release any trapped bubbles.

IMPORTANT: The longer you mix, the faster the plaster will set. Overmixing can cause the plaster to set up before you have a chance to pour it into the mold.

5. Pour Mixture into Mold.
Pour the plaster slowly to prevent air bubbles until the mold is full. (Photo 2) Gently shake the mold to help loosen air bubbles and level the top of the casting. Let set 10 to 15 minutes. IMPORTANT: **Never** pour excess plaster down a drain. Allow the plaster to harden in the mixing bowl, then flex to remove. Cured plaster can be thrown away in household trash.

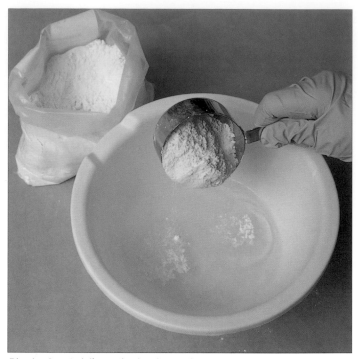
Photo 1 – Adding plaster to water.

Photo 2 – Pouring plaster into a mold.

6. **Add a Hanger.** *Optional:*
Include this step if you are planning to hang your casting. When the plaster has set a bit, add a sawtooth hanger at the top of the casting. The plaster should be able to hold the hanger without falling to the bottom of the mold.

7. **Let Plaster Set and Harden.**
Allow the plaster to sit undisturbed so it will harden. When the plaster has set (I prefer to wait until the next day) and the water on top has evaporated, the casting is ready to remove from the mold.

8. **Remove the Casting from the Mold.**
Cover a surface (such as a table or counter) with old towels.
From a plastic mold: Gently flex the mold to loosen the casting. Place the casting on the flat, soft surface. and gently lift the mold off the casting.
From a latex rubber mold: Place the mold on a soft, flat surface. Carefully remove the backup shell. Grasp the latex mold and stretch it gently off the casting on all edges. Carefully peel the latex mold away from the casting. (Photo 3)
From a sand mold: Dig the sand away from the casting and gently lift it out of the container.

9. **Trim the Casting.**
Use a plaster knife to trim the sharp edge of the casting. Use the rough side of a moist sanding sponge to smooth the trimmed areas. (Photo 4) Brush away the excess with the sponge.

10. **Allow to Dry Completely.**
At this stage, the casting is still very wet, is light gray in color, and needs to dry further. (When completely dry, the plaster will be bright white.) Place the casting on a wire rack so the air can circulate. (Using an electric fan speeds up the process.) Large castings may take several days to dry completely.

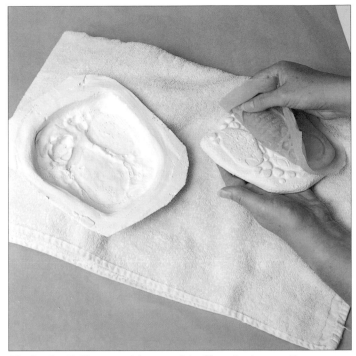

Photo 3 – Pulling a rubber mold off a plaster casting.

Photo 4 – Smoothing the edges of a plaster casting with a sanding sponge.

Painting the Plaster Casting

paints & finishes

- **Acrylic Craft Paints:** I prefer to use acrylic paints on plaster castings. They come in a wide range of colors and can be used to create a variety of different decorative finishes. While still wet, acrylic paints and mediums clean up easily with soap and water. When dry and cured, they are durable and waterproof.
- **Acrylic All-purpose Sealer** can be used to seal the unpainted surface of the plaster if it is a particularly porous type of plaster. This sealer can also be used to protect the painted surface of the casting.
- **Antiquing Glaze, or Gel Stain Medium** also can be used after the item is painted to add definition to the painting.
- **Acrylic Varnishes** come in gloss, satin, and matte finishes as well as sepia, metallic, and iridescent tones. These are used to protect the surface after the piece is painted.

basic painting supplies

- **Paint brushes**, for applying paint, mediums, and sealers

- **Paper towels, water basin, and brush cleaner soap** for cleaning brushes.

painting techniques

These simple techniques can be used alone or combined to create a variety of finishes. After you master the techniques, follow the finishing recipes to create many looks, including old weathered bronze and tarnished silver.

Sealing – Plaster castings should be sealed before painting to prevent them from absorbing moisture from the air. To prepare, remove any dust. Use an acrylic sealer to coat the completely dry plaster casting. Let the sealant dry completely before proceeding.

Basecoating – A properly applied coat of **acrylic paint** creates a base for decorative finishes. Apply the first coat of acrylic color with a large brush to evenly coat the surface with paint, and let dry completely. Add another coat of paint, then a third coat (if needed) to cover the surface evenly. There should be no patches or visible brush marks.

Color Washing – Place equal parts **gel stain medium** and acrylic paint on a palette. Mix well with a palette knife. With your brush, apply the mix to the surface to one area of the casting at a time, getting into all the crevices and details. Use a soft cloth to remove the excess from the raised areas of the casting and highlight the recesses by placing a different color there.

Dry Brushing – Dry brushing highlights the raised areas of the casting with a thin layer of paint. Place a small amount of full strength **acrylic paint** on your brush. Remove most of the paint from the brush by stroking it on a paper towel. Brush lightly over the raised areas of the casting.

Metallic Highlighting – As in dry brushing, metallic highlighting adds color to raised areas. **Metallic wax paste** comes in tubes and pots – it's easy to use and gives the casting a beautiful, tarnish-free metallic accent. Use you finger to apply the paste.

Pearl Highlighting – **Pearl powders** can be rubbed on castings for a pearlized finish. Wrap your finger with a piece of paper towel, dip in the powder, and shake off the excess. Rub the casting to apply the powder.

Finishing – Properly protecting your finished work means it will last for years of enjoyment. On painted castings, apply two or three coats of acrylic **varnish**. Roll, don't shake the varnish container to minimize bubbles on your finished piece. Pour the varnish in a small disposable bowl (to prevent the large container from being contaminated). Use a large, soft brush to apply the varnish in slow, thin coats. Let each coat dry thoroughly before adding another layer.

Basecoating   Color washing   Dry brushing   Metallic highlighting

recipes for painted finishes on plaster

- **Tarnished Silver** (#1 in photo) – Clear sealer, metallic silver basecoat, black color wash

- **Gold Leaf Look** (#2 in photo) – Clear sealer, terra cotta basecoat, gold metallic paste highlights

- **Rust** (#3 in photo) – Clear sealer, terra cotta basecoat sprinkled with fine sand while paint is still wet, dark brown color wash, gray-blue dry brushing

- **Pewter** (#4 in photo) – Clear sealer, metallic silver basecoat, black color wash, white dry brushing

- **Pearl** (#5 in photo) – Clear sealer, white basecoat, pearl buffing powder

- **Verdigris** (#6 in photo) – Clear sealer, dark green basecoat, patina (light turquoise) color wash, gold metallic paste highlights (Use copper or bronze metallic paste for different weathered metal effects.)

- **Terra Cotta** (#7 in photo) – Clear sealer, terra cotta basecoat, white color wash

- **Antique Ivory** (#8 in photo) – Clear sealer, light ivory basecoat, brown color glaze, pearl buffing powder

- **Aged** (#9 in photo) – Clear sealer, light ivory basecoat, brown color wash, gold metallic paste highlights

Floral Table Accessories

These pastel posies were cast in candy molds – a variety of coordinating motifs are available. Use them as placecard holders, to make napkin rings, or to decorate glass votive holders.

supplies

Casting plaster

Water

Floral-motif candy molds

Surfactant

Acrylic craft paints – Pale yellow, baby blue, pink, white

Pearl powder

Glue gun and clear glue sticks

White craft glue

Clear glass votive holder

Green wire-edge ribbon, 1-1/2" wide, 14" for each napkin ring

30 gauge beading wire

20 gauge copper wire, 10" for each placecard holder

Green vellum (for leaves)

Equipment from list of Basic Supplies. (See page 84.)

instructions

Make the Flowers:

1. Mix and pour the plaster according to the instructions in "Plaster Casting, Step by Step" at the beginning of this section. Let set.
2. Unmold when set. Trim and smooth castings as needed. Let dry completely.
3. Basecoat the flowers with pink, yellow, and blue acrylic paints.
4. Dry brush the pieces with white paint. See "Painting Techniques." Let dry.
5. Polish with pearl powder to give the flowers a soft luster.

To Create a Placecard Holder:

1. Coil a 14" piece of copper wire at each end.
2. Use glue to attach one coil to the back of the plaster flower. Let dry.
3. When the glue is dry, bend the wire to create the stand.
4. Cut leaves from green vellum. Attached to the back of the flower by slipping into the wire coil.

To Create a Napkin Ring:

1. Fold under 2" of each end of a 14" piece of ribbon to create a 10" piece.
2. Fold the ribbon in half lengthwise. Secure with beading wire 1-3/4" from the turned-under ends. (This will form the ring and the bow loops.)
3. Open the bow loops. Hot glue the plaster flower in the center.

To Decorate a Votive Holder:

1. Form a two-loop bow and secure the center with wire.
2. Use the glue gun to attach a strip of green vellum around the top of the votive holder.
3. Glue the bow to the holder, then glue the plaster flower at the center of the bow.
4. Add water so the holder is three-quarters full. Place a white floating votive candle in the water. ❑

Picture Bow

This project shows how a plaster casting can serve as a decorative accent for a picture bow.
You can change the colors to coordinate with any color scheme.

Picture Bow

supplies

Casting plaster

Water

Angel plaster mold

Acrylic craft paint – Terra cotta

Metallic paste – Gold

Glue gun and clear glue sticks

1-1/2 yds. peach wire-edge ribbon, 1-1/2" wide

1 yd. sheer peach ribbon, 1-1/2" wide

1/2 yd. *each* of two coordinating satin ribbons, 1/2" wide

30 gauge beading wire

Needle and peach thread

Equipment from list of Basic Supplies. (See page 84.)

instructions

1. Mix and pour the plaster to make the casting according to the instructions in "Plaster Casting, Step by Step" at the beginning of this section. Let set.
2. Unmold when set.
3. Trim and smooth the edges as needed. Let dry completely.
4. Apply a gold leaf painted finish, following the Painting Recipe in this section. Let dry.
5. Make a large 6-loop bow with peach wire-edge ribbon and a 6-loop bow with peach sheer ribbon. Secure the centers of the bows with beading wire.
6. Reserve 4" of satin ribbon for a hanger and make two small 4-loop bows with the satin ribbons. Secure the centers of the bows with beading wire.
7. Glue the bows in place with the casting in the center, using the photo as a guide.
8. Make a small loop with the 4" piece of satin ribbon. Sew to the back for a hanger. ❏

Bow Wall Ornament

Pictured on page 94

supplies

Casting plaster

Water

Angel plaster mold

Acrylic craft paint – Light green

Pearl powder

Glue gun and clear glue sticks

1-1/2 yds. green wire-edge ribbon, 1-1/2" wide

1 yd. green satin ribbon, 1/2" wide

1/2 yd. *each* of two green checked ribbons, 1/2" wide

30 gauge beading wire

Large painted wooden letter with a gold eye hook attached to the top center

Needle and green thread

Equipment from list of Basic Supplies. (See page 84.)

instructions

1. Mix and pour the plaster to make the casting according to the instructions in "Plaster Casting, Step by Step" at the beginning of this section. Let set.
2. Unmold when set.
3. Trim and smooth the edges as needed. Let dry completely.
4. Paint the casting with green paint. Let dry.
5. Highlight the painted surface with pearl powder.
6. Reserve a 4" piece of green satin ribbon. Make a large 6-loop bow with green wire-edge ribbon and a large 6-loop bow with the green satin ribbon. Secure the centers with wire.
7. Make a small 4-loop bow with one of the checked ribbons. Secure the center with wire.
8. Attach the letter by making a loop with the other checked ribbon and threading it through the eye hook and around the large bow. With the remaining checked ribbon, make a small bow and glue at the top of the letter.
9. Using the photo as a guide, glue the bows and the casting together with the casting in the center.
10. Make a loop with the 4" piece of satin ribbon. Sew to the back of the bow for a hanger. ❏

Bow Wall Ornament

Bows can become a decorative background for attaching plaster pieces for a wall ornament.
Choose a ribbon color to match your décor.

Lace Angel

This delightful angel hangs on the wall to accent a Victorian-theme room. It could also be attached to a piece of furniture.

supplies

Casting plaster

Water

Angel plaster mold

Surfactant

Acrylic craft paint – Light ivory

Antiquing glaze – Brown

Metallic paste – gold

Glue gun and clear glue sticks

Round crocheted dollies, 2" and 6" diameter

1 lace applique

4 ivory ribbon roses

Ivory satin ribbon, 1/4" wide

Gold cherub button

Gold and pearl beads, various sizes

Sawtooth hanger

Equipment from list of Basic Supplies. (See page 84.)

instructions

1. Mix and pour the plaster to make the casting according to the instructions in "Plaster Casting, Step by Step" at the beginning of this section. Let set up a bit.
2. Place a sawtooth hanger in the plaster according to the instructions in "Plaster Casting, Step by Step." Let set.
3. Unmold when set. Trim and smooth the edges as needed. Let dry completely.
4. Apply an aged painted finish, following the Painting Recipe in this section. Let dry.
5. Glue the small doily to the back of the angel's head to create the lacy halo.
6. Cut and glue the larger doily to the bottom of the wings.
7. Glue the applique to the large doily.
8. Make bows with the ivory ribbon, leaving long tails.
9. Glue the ribbon roses, ribbon bows and tails, cherub button, and beads to the doily in a pleasing cluster at the center to accent, using the photo as a guide. Glue additional beads around the bottom of the angel. ❑

Rusted Gargoyle Vase

A plaster casting is a simple way to add ornamentation to a vase. You can use this technique to add cast motifs to lampshades, furniture, and frames.

supplies

Casting plaster

Water

Gargoyle soap mold

Surfactant

Acrylic craft paints – Terra cotta, light gray-blue

Antiquing glaze – Dark brown

Fine sand

White craft glue

Vase with flat sides. (Mine is antique white with crackle glaze.)

Equipment from list of Basic Supplies. (See page 84.)

instructions

1. Mix and pour the plaster to make two gargoyles according to the instructions in "Plaster Casting, Step by Step" at the beginning of this section. Let set.
2. Unmold. Trim and smooth as needed. Let dry completely.
3. Seal the gargoyles. Let dry.
4. Apply a painted rust finish, following the Painting Recipe in this section. Let dry.
5. Glue a gargoyle on the back and front of the vase. ❏

Silver Claddagh Box

This pretty box is accented with a plaster claddagh, the Irish symbol of love, loyalty, and friendship.

supplies

Casting plaster

Water

Claddagh motif soap mold

Surfactant

Acrylic craft paints – Black, metallic silver

Antiquing glaze – Black

Metallic paste – Ruby

White craft glue

Wooden box

Silver box corners

Silver frame charm

Round silver motif

Acrylic varnish

Equipment from list of Basic Supplies. (See page 84.)

instructions

1. Mix and pour the plaster to make one claddagh casting according to the instructions in "Plaster Casting, Step by Step" at the beginning of this section. Let set.
2. Unmold. Trim and smooth as needed. Let dry completely.
3. Basecoat the box with black. Apply as many coats as needed for complete coverage. Let dry.
4. Using white glue, glue the plaster casting to the top of the box.
5. Glue the silver frame charm around the casting. Let dry.
6. Paint the plaster casting and the area inside the frame with silver metallic paint. Let dry.
7. Apply black glaze to the painted surface. Wipe, leaving the glaze in the crevices. Let dry.
8. With ruby metallic paste, highlight the heart in the casting.
9. Varnish the box.
10. Glue the metal corners in place.

11. On the front of the box, attach the round motif to the lid with glue. Make sure only the top part is glued to the surface so the box will open. ❑

Celtic Knot Frame

Plaster castings add dramatic impact to an ordinary wooden frame. Choose a flat frame as wide as the size of the finished castings.

supplies

Casting plaster

Water

Celtic knot soap molds

Surfactant

Acrylic craft paint – Dark green

Antiquing glaze – Light turquoise

Acrylic stain – Brown

Gold metallic paste

White craft glue

Wooden frame

Equipment from list of Basic Supplies. (See page 84.)

instructions

1. Mix and pour the plaster to make four Celtic knots according to the instructions in "Plaster Casting, Step by Step" at the beginning of this section. Let set.
2. Unmold. Trim and smooth as needed. Let dry completely.
3. Stain the wooden frame dark brown. Let dry.
4. Seal the castings. Let dry.
5. Apply a verdigris painted finish, following the Painting Recipe in this section. Let dry.
6. Glue the plaster castings to the corners of the frame. ❏

Fruit Plaque

I created this design using plastic fruit and silk flower leaves. A master was made of the piece to create the casting. The mold master was made with oil-based clay and decorated with rubber stamps. The technique can be duplicated with other plastic fruits to create a series of decorative tiles. This painted casting makes an impressive tile with the look of aged metal.

supplies

Casting plaster

Water

Sawtooth hanger

Equipment from list of Basic Supplies. (See page 84.)

For the mold:

Supplies for making a mold master (See "Creating a Master" in the Techniques section.)

Glass mosaic pieces; 1/2" and 1" squares and 1/2" flat marbles

Rubber stamps – Crackle texture, small alphabet letters

Small plastic pear

Silk or real leaves

Rubber latex mold builder

Glue brush

Plaster cloth

Sharp knife

For decorating:

Acrylic craft paint – Dark green

Antiquing glaze – Light turquoise

Metallic paste – Gold

instructions

Make the Mold:

1. Create a 4" square plaque from oil-based clay.
2. Texture the edges of the plaque with the crackle stamp.
3. Position the plastic pear. Cut out a space in the clay base so three-quarters of the pear is visible.
4. Roll out some clay 1/4" thick. Press in the leaf. Cut out the leaf with a sharp knife and place on the tile. Make another clay leaf and drape over the edge of the tile, using the photo as a guide for placement. Trim.
5. Stamp the word PEAR, using alphabet stamps.
6. Make the latex mold and a backup mold according to the instructions in the Techniques section.

Cast and Decorate:

1. The mold was supported in sand for pouring. Mix and pour the plaster to make the casting according to the instructions in "Plaster Casting, Step by Step" at the beginning of this section. Let set up a bit.

2. Place a sawtooth hanger in the plaster at the top of the plaque according to the instructions in "Plaster Casting, Step by Step." Let set.

3. Unmold when set. Trim and smooth the edges as needed. Let dry completely.

4. Apply a verdigris painted finish, following the Painting Recipe in this section. Let dry.

Sidewalk Chalk

This simple project is perfect for a first plaster casting experience because bubbles and slight mars on the pieces don't matter. It's also a fun project to do with children. I recommend you use the less expensive plaster of Paris instead of a casting plaster. You can find tempera powder in the children's art supplies section of crafts and art supply stores. (This colors the plaster and creates the colored chalk.)

supplies

Plaster of Paris

Water

Tempera paint powder

Plastic soap molds with large cavities and simple shapes

Surfactant

Equipment from list of Basic Supplies. (See page 84.)

instructions

1. To every 1/2 cup of dry plaster, add a heaping tablespoon of powdered tempera paint. Mix well. Add more or less to vary the hues.
2. Mix and pour the plaster in your prepared molds according to the instructions in "Plaster Casting, Step by Step" at the beginning of this section. Let set for a day before unmolding.
3. Trim as needed. NOTE: The chalk will be moist but can be used right away. *Option:* Let it dry an extra day before using. ❏

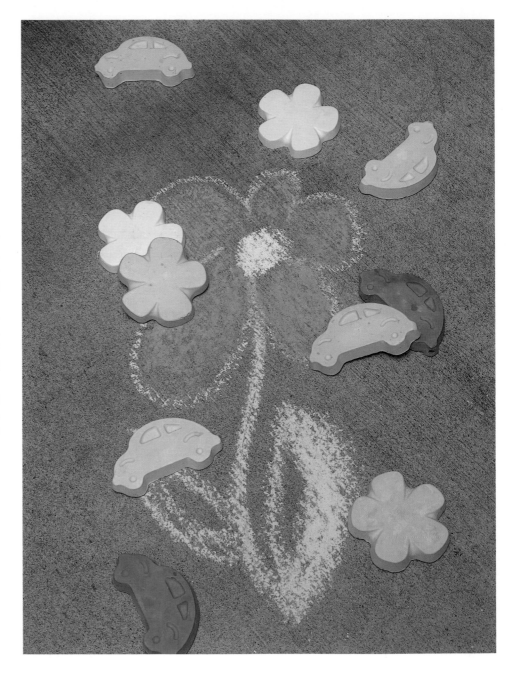

Mosaic Mirror Frame

This rustic, Moroccan inspired mirror was created with a sand mold.

supplies

Casting plaster

Water

Plastic container, at least 12" square

Fine sand

Acrylic craft paints – Terra cotta, moss green

Antiquing glaze – White

Mosaic pieces, 1/2" and 1" squares – Mirror, blue tiles, green tiles

Mirror, 3" square

3" square mold *or* 3" square cardboard box

Sawtooth hanger

Trowel

Small scoop

Equipment from list of Basic Supplies. (See page 84.)

instructions

1. Put the sand in the plastic container. Dampen the sand.
2. Prepare the mold by digging a hole 9" x 9" x 3" deep in the damp sand. Smooth the sides and the bottom with a trowel. It does not need to be perfect – the irregularities of a hand-built mold are part of the frame's rustic charm.
3. Pack the 3" square mold (or any other square box) with sand and unmold in the center of the cavity (just like building castles in the sand at the beach).
4. Place the mirror face down on the square sand molding. (This places the mirror in the frame in the finished casting.)
5. Arrange the mosaic pieces around the cavity in an irregular pattern, using the photo as a guide. **Do not** push the pieces into the sand.
6. Mix and pour the plaster to make the casting according to the instructions in "Plaster Casting, Step by Step" at the beginning of this section. Use a small scoop to carefully place and pour the plaster into the mold to avoid moving the mosaic pieces. Let set up a bit.
7. Place a sawtooth hanger in the plaster according to the instructions in "Plaster Casting, Step by Step" at the beginning of this section. Let set completely.
8. Unmold. Remove the excess sand by rinsing the frame under water. Let dry completely.
9. Basecoat the frame with the terra cotta paint, avoiding the mirror and tile pieces.
10. Color wash with white glaze for a terra cotta finish.
11. Dry brush with green paint for a mossy, aged appearance. Wipe away any paint from the mosaic pieces and mirror. ❏

Inspiration Plaque

Let a word or your hobby inspire you to create a plaque for your workspace. A mold master was made with oil-based clay and other items attached to it.

supplies

Casting plaster

Water

Equipment from list of Basic Supplies. (See page 84.)

For the mold:

Supplies for making a mold master (See "Creating a Master" in the Techniques section.)

Glass mosaic pieces – 1/2" and 1" squares, 1/2" flat marbles

Rubber stamps – Crackle texture, Medieval script, large and small alphabets

Fleur de lis charms

Metal key

Polymer clay molds

Rubber latex mold builder

Glue brush

Plaster cloth

For decorating:

Acrylic craft paints – Ivory, black, tan

Antiquing glaze – Brown

Metallic paste – Gold

instructions

Make the Mold:

1. Create the master, latex mold, and back-up mold according to the instructions in the Techniques section to create a 5" x 6" plaque.
2. Texture the edges of the plaque with the crackle stamp.
3. Roll out a 2" x 3" oval piece of clay. Stamp with the script stamp. Place on the clay base.
4. Position the mosaic pieces, metal key, and charms on the base and press into the clay.
5. Impress the word ART with the large letter stamps and the word CREATE with the small letter stamps.
6. Push oil-based clay into polymer clay molds to create the faces and angel. Unmold and place on the base.

Cast and Decorate:

1. When the mold is complete, mix and pour the plaster to make the casting according to the instructions in "Plaster Casting, Step by Step" at the beginning of this section. Let set up a bit.
2. Place a sawtooth hanger in the plaster at the top of the plaque according to the instructions in "Plaster Casting, Step by Step." Let set.
3. Unmold when set. Trim and smooth the edges as needed. Let dry completely.
4. Basecoat the entire plaque with ivory.
5. Paint the square mosaic pieces, the raised script area, and the word ART with black paint.
6. Paint the key and cherub with tan paint.
7. Dry brush the black raised script area with tan paint.
8. Antique the entire plaque with brown glaze to bring out the details.
9. With gold metallic paste, highlight the faces, the key, and the fleur de lis motifs. ❏

Frog Plaque

A mold master was made for this piece. The base of the mold master was made with oil-based clay and decorated with found materials and rubber stamps. This nature-inspired plaque is a perfect tabletop companion to a houseplant.

supplies

Casting plaster

Water

Sawtooth hanger

Equipment from list of Basic Supplies. (See page 84.)

For the mold:

Supplies for making a mold master (See "Creating a Master" in the Techniques section.)

Plastic toy frog

Pebbles

Rubber stamps – Crackle texture, Medieval script

Rubber latex mold builder

Glue brush

Plaster cloth

For decorating:

Acrylic craft paints – Ivory, black, green

Antiquing glaze – Brown

Metallic paste – Gold

instructions

Make the Mold:

1. Create a 5" x 6" plaque from oil-based clay.
2. Texture the edges of the plaque with the crackle stamp.
3. Roll out two pieces of clay to make 3" to 4" ovals. Stamp with the script stamp. Place on the clay base.
4. Position the plastic frog and press into the clay.
5. Press in the pebbles around the edges to finish the master.
6. Make the latex mold and backup mold according to the instructions in the Techniques section.

Cast and Decorate:

1. When the mold is complete, mix and pour the plaster to make the casting according to the instructions in "Plaster Casting, Step by Step" at the beginning of this section. Let set up a bit.
2. Place a sawtooth hanger in the plaster at the top of the plaque according to the instructions in "Plaster Casting, Step by Step." Let set.
3. Unmold when set. Trim and smooth the edges as needed. Let dry completely.
4. Basecoat the entire plaque with ivory.
5. Paint the raised script areas with black.
6. Paint the frog with green.
7. Antique the entire plaque with brown glaze to bring out the details.
8. Dry brush the sides of the plaque with green paint to give a mossy appearance.
9. With gold metallic paste, highlight the black script ovals. ❏

Cement or Concrete?

Cement is a dry powder; concrete is the finished product. Cement is only cement as long as it remains dry and loose. If you leave a bag of cement in the garden shed and it absorbs moisture and becomes solid, you have concrete, not cement.

Cement Casting

techniques & projects

Working with cement to make castings for your garden is a little more work than casting with plaster. Cement is heavy to mix, but mixing is an important step. Having a helper makes the job easier. The most difficult part of the process is waiting for the concrete to cure so you can use your casting! The results are waterproof, long lasting, and can remain outdoors year-round.

All mortars, grout, vinyl patch concrete, and pre-mixed cement are cement mixed with a variety of aggregates. Concrete is sand or gravel held together by solidified gypsum. Concrete structures – such as the Roman Pantheon – can last for thousands of years.

Casting the Piece

cement

The main ingredient in modern concrete is Portland cement, which is used in all the projects along with added aggregates, such as sand or gravel. Portland cement is finely ground mineral powder that undergoes a chemical reaction when mixed with water. Thorough mixing of cement, aggregate, and water is important – as it dries and cures, the cement crystallizes around the aggregate, and the resulting concrete is strong and durable. Cement cannot be used alone for casting – it will be brittle and will break easily.

TIPS

- Do not mix plaster with cement; this results in a soft mixture that is not waterproof.
- Do not use concrete mixes for casting projects. Use Portland cement and add your own aggregates.
- Do not use beach sand as an aggregate – it contains too much salt and may hinder the curing of the concrete.
- Store unused cement powder in a sealed bag. Exposed cement absorbs moisture and will harden over time.
- Because cement is heavy, choose a worksite where you can mix, pour, and let your casting cure.
- When using plastic molds, fill them in the location where they will be curing. If you try to move a filled mold, it could break.
- It's best to let your castings set at above 50 degrees F.

cement casting basic supplies

- **Portland cement**, for bonding

- **Aggregate**, such as gravel or sand, for strength

- **Bucket with water**

- **Molds**, including plastic molds designed for cement casting, plaster molds, plastic plant saucers

- **Mold release**, such as petroleum jelly, vegetable oil, or mineral oil

- **Inexpensive paint brush**, for applying mold release

- **Paper towels**, for removing excess mold release

- **Surfactant** as a mold release

- **Cement pigments**, for tinting. Find them at hardware, crafts, or art supply stores in powder and liquid forms.

- **Wire mesh**, for reinforcing the concrete to decrease the chance of cracking. Readily available in rolls at home improvement centers.

- **Wire cutters**, for cutting the wire mesh

equipment for each project

- **Wheelbarrow** (for large batches) or **plastic tub** (for small batches), for mixing the cement

- **One-quart plastic container**, to use as a scoop to measure ingredients

- **Trowel**, for mixing, moving, and smoothing the mixed cement

- **Garden hoe**, for mixing larger batches

- **Rubber gloves**, to protect your hands (Cement is a skin irritant – wear gloves to protect your hands from excessive drying and burns.)

- **Dust mask**, to protect your lungs from irritating cement dust

- **Plastic sheeting**, to protect your work area and to drape freshly poured cement (Black plastic trash bags, cut open, work well.)

cement casting supplies & equipment

1. Water bucket, 2. Large mixing container, 3. Mold, 4. Mold release (oil) and brush,
5. Trowel, 6. Cement pigments, 7. Portland cement, 8. Sand, 9. Rubber gloves,
10. Wire mesh reinforcement, 11. Wire cutters, 12. Plastic trash bag

cement casting, step by step

1. Apply the Mold Release.

Brush all the mold surfaces with petroleum jelly or oil, using an inexpensive brush. Remove the excess with a paper towel. (You need only a thin film.) NOTE: You will be able to paint on the cured concrete. The oil is absorbed into the casting and there are no paint adhesion problems, even with acrylic paints.

2. Measure and Mix the Dry Ingredients.

I used two parts sand to one part Portland cement for this stepping stone. In a wheelbarrow or utility tub, blend the dry cement and aggregate together well. If using powdered pigments, add them now. TIP: Record how much pigment was added in case you want to duplicate the color in future castings.

3. Add Water and Mix.

Mixing is a very important, strategic step.

Add one part water and stir well. Add more water, if needed, to create a mix resembling thick muffin batter – it should be pourable, but very thick. If using liquid pigments, add them now. Mix long enough to completely incorporate all the ingredients without any dry spots remaining. (Photo 1)

• Err on the side of a thicker mix, as you can always add more water.

• If you add too much water, sprinkle in some dry cement to get the perfect consistency.

• Use a wheelbarrow and a garden hoe for mixing larger batches.

• There's no need to hurry when mixing cement. It takes a while to set.

4. Spray Mold with Surfactant.

Spray a surfactant into the mold right before you start to pour in the cement. This helps to avoid air bubbles on the surface of your casting. You can also use ammonia or window cleaner to reduce surface tension on mold surfaces when casting cement.

5. Fill the Mold.

Fill the prepared mold above one-third full by pouring the concrete from the mixing container or using a shovel or trowel. (Photo 2) Gently shake or tap the mold on the ground to remove air bubbles. (This also allows the mix to better settle into the detailed surface of the mold.) If you are using wire reinforcement, place it in the mold. Fill the mold to 1/4" from the top, covering the wire. Gently shake to level the cement. For easy clean-up, immediately rinse your mixing tub or wheelbarrow and trowel or hoe in water.

Photo 1 – Mixing cement to make a stepping stone.

Photo 2 – Pouring the mixed cement into a prepared plastic mold.

6. Add a Hanger, *Option:*
If you plan to hang the casting, place a sawtooth hanger on the back when the cement can support the weight (after it has cured 5 to 10 minutes).

7. Cover and Let Cure.
Cover your mold with plastic and allow to cure undisturbed for 48 hours. Don't let the surface of the concrete dry out – mist it regularly with water to keep it damp.

8. Remove from the Mold.
When ready to unmold, lay the mold (concrete side down) on a soft surface, such as grassy ground or a stack of old towels. Flex the edges of the mold and push the top of the mold gently until you feel the vacuum break. Carefully lift the mold off the casting. (Photo 3)

9. Allow to Cure Fully.
Allow the casting to cure for another week before adding surface finishes such as stain or paint. Concrete can take up to 28 days to reach its maximum strength.

Photo 3 – Remove the stepping stone from the mold.

Decorating the Piece

sealants
Sealants can be added to the cement mix or brushed on after the cement has cured. Look for sealant products that are designed to be added to the concrete mix before pouring, or brush clear acrylic sealant on the casting after it has completely cured. Epoxy coatings can be used on concrete or hypertufa projects for better water retention.

stains & washes
You can enhance your casting with a stain or a wash. A wash can be applied as soon as the casting has been released from the mold. For an easy wash, mix Portland cement, water, and concrete pigment into a thin slurry (it should be thin enough to apply with a brush). Mix the slurry and brush over the casting. Wipe the slurry off the high relief areas with a towel to accentuate the dimensional aspects. Let the casting cure fully, then add a sealant.

paints
Outdoor acrylic craft paint can be used to paint cured concrete castings. Cleanup is easy with soap and water and the paint is waterproof when dry.

creating a mossy finish
You can encourage moss and lichen to grow on concrete or hypertufa items, but this can take a long time. To speed up the process, put a handful of moss in a blender with some buttermilk and blend to make a thick slurry. Brush on the newly unmolded casting, mist with water, and place in shady location. If you maintain a consistent dampness on the surface, you will soon have a lovely mossy patina that makes your casting look like it has been in the garden for years.

adding decorative accents
Use decorative items to add interest to castings. After pouring the cement:
- Wait 5 to 10 minutes to decorate with objects such as pebbles, shells, and mosaic pieces. (This is also when to add a sawtooth hanger if you wish to create a hanging plaque.)
- Wait 10 to 20 minutes to write or draw in the concrete. Use a wooden craft stick or press plastic letters in the surface. If the concrete seems to collapse in or the impressions aren't clear and sharp impression, wait a little longer.
- Wait 30 minutes to make handprints or footprints in the wet concrete. Rinse the concrete from hands and feet immediately. TIP: Use a good barrier cream to avoid dry or irritated skin from the caustic uncured concrete.

Garden Edgers

There are beautiful molds available for casting your own decorative garden edging.
I recommend you buy three or four molds to make the job go faster.
To make them, follow the instructions for "Cement Casting, Step by Step" at the beginning of
this section. When the edgers are fully cured, dig a 4" trough at the edge of your planting bed.
Place the edgers in the trough, level, and pack soil around them to hold them in place.

Grape Stepping Stones

You'll find a variety of plastic stepping stone molds – both plain and detailed. To make stepping stones, follow the instructions for "Cement Casting, Step by Step" at the beginning of this section. The stones pictured below are made from the same mold but are graduated in color. A little less pigment was added to each batch to create this varied effect. After being released from the molds, they were washed with a cement, pigment, and water slurry to bring out the details.

Pebble Mosaic Stepping Stones

Stepping stones are an ideal summer project to make with children. I used plastic 10" round planter saucers as molds for these stepping stones. To make them, follow the instructions for "Cement Casting, Step by Step" at the beginning of this section. Pour the cement in the molds and level with a trowel. Wait 5 to 10 minutes, then push pebbles in a spiral design into the fresh cement, partly submerging them to ensure they are firmly held in place.

Planter Feet

You can purchase molds to make planter feet or use large soap molds to create multiple castings of the same motif. Here, a frog mold was used to make these planter supports for a hypertufa planter. Green pigment was used to color the concrete.

To make them, follow the instructions for "Cement Casting, Step by Step" at the beginning of this section. Pour the cement in the molds and level with a trowel.

Saying Stones

Make your own walk of fame with handprints and family names or create garden poetry that will last for decades. The supplies to make these stones come in a kit that includes molds of different sizes, plastic letters to imprint the wet concrete, a trowel, and enough cement to make a few stones, but you could easily assemble the supplies to make your own kit. To cast these stones, I used a vinyl patch concrete mix that contains a fine sand aggregate that allows for sharp details. The 40 lb. bag makes 12 to 15 medium-size stones.

If you make a thicker consistency mix, as the plastic frame molds are filled, leveled, marked with the plastic letters, you can remove the mold right away. Because you are unmolding them as you go, you can make lots of stones at once. To make them, prepare a work area with plastic sheeting and follow the instructions for "Cement Casting, Step by Step" at the beginning of this section.

Hypertufa Casting

techniques & projects

Planters made with hypertufa have a natural, rugged look that complements plants and shrubs in the garden. Hypertufa pots are very plant-friendly – the porous walls act as a reservoir for water and provide good air flow to root systems. Hypertufa can be poured into molds to make stepping stones or formed in sand molds to fashion birdbaths, fountains, or hanging accents. As hypertufa castings age in the garden, the peat will weather out and leave the surface pitted and porous, which adds to the aged effect.

Techniques & Projects

hypertufa

Hypertufa is the synthetic version of tufa rock, a spongy rock found in limestone quarries and along coastlines. For centuries, tufa rock has been hollowed out and used for water basins, tubs, and planters.

The basic techniques for casting hypertufa are the same as the techniques for concrete, but using different aggregates makes the finished projects lighter and more rustic. There are many recipes for hypertufa stone – a basic mixture usually consists of Portland cement, sand, peat moss, and vermiculite or perlite.

hypertufa, basic supplies

- **Portland cement,** the amount for the casting

- **Sand**

- **Peat moss**

- **Perlite and/or vermiculite** – Both are soil conditioners and available at garden centers.

- **Bucket with water**

- **Molds or container with sand,** including plastic molds designed for cement casting, plaster molds, plastic plant saucers

- **Mold release,** such as petroleum jelly, vegetable oil, or mineral oil

- **Inexpensive paint brush,** for applying mold release

- **Paper towels,** for removing excess mold release

- **Surfactant** as a mold release

- **Cement pigments,** for tinting. Find them at hardware, crafts, or art supply stores in powder and liquid forms.

- **Wire mesh,** for reinforcing the concrete to decrease the chance of cracking. Readily available in rolls at home improvement centers.

- **Wire cutters,** for cutting the wire mesh

- **Tubes for drainage holes** – I used plastic bottles such as plastic film containers – cut off the top and bottom to form a 1-1/2" tall plastic tube

- **Tamping stick** – A piece of wood (like a shim or cedar shingle) or a wooden dowel, to tamp down the mixture in the mold.

equipment for every project

- **Wheelbarrow** (for large batches) or **plastic tub** (for small batches), for mixing the cement

- **One-quart plastic container,** to use as a scoop to measure ingredients

- **Trowel,** for mixing, moving, and smoothing the mixed cement

- **Garden hoe,** for mixing larger batches

- **Rubber gloves,** to protect your hands (Cement is a skin irritant – wear gloves to protect your hands from excessive drying and burns.)

- **Dust mask,** to protect your lungs from irritating cement dust

- **Plastic sheeting,** to protect your work area and to drape freshly poured cement (Black plastic trash bags, cut open, work well.)

hypertufa supplies & tools

1. Peat moss, 2. Perlite, 3. Portland cement, 4. Sand, 5. Vermiculite, 6. Tamping board, 7. Drainage hole tubes

hypertufa casting, step by step

As an example, we are making a **round planter** as shown in photo. For this round planter you will need two plastic bowls, one larger and one with smaller overall dimensions by at least 1". I used very inexpensive plastic nesting bowls from the dollar store.

1. Prepare the Molds.
With the inside bowl, I trimmed the top rim off. For this size of planter, one drainage hole tube will be sufficient. Prepare the inside of the larger bowl and the outside of the smaller bowl with mold release.

2. Mix the Dry Ingredients.
Mix one part peat moss, one part vermiculite or perlite, one part sand, and one part Portland cement. Mix well.

3. Add Water.
Add sufficient water to make a stiff mixture, not runny and able to hold its shape.

4. Place the Drainage Tube.
You need a drainage hole if you are making a planter; other hypertufa castings may not require drainage holes.

Stand the drainage tube upright on the bottom of the larger bowl. Place a layer of the hypertufa mix in and around the drainage plug in the bowl, tamping down the layer as you go.

5. Position the Smaller Bowl.

Place the smaller bowl on the hypertufa mix in the bottom of the larger bowl. Make sure there is equal space between the bowls on all sides.

6. Fill the Space.

Fill the space between the bowls, using the tamping stick to push the mix down and remove air bubbles. (Photo 1) Fill the smaller bowl with sand – this will keep the smaller bowl in place.

7. Let Set.

Let set at least 48 hours. **Do not** move or tip the planter at this stage. Sprinkle lightly with water after molding and keep it moist during the curing process.

8. Remove from the Molds.

After the hypertufa has set, remove the inside bowl. (Photo 2) It's best to turn the large bowl over a soft surface, such as the grassy ground or piles of old towels, to prevent cracking. Gently flex the outer bowl to break the vacuum. Remove the outer bowl.

9. *Option:* Apply a Mossy Finish.

You can brush on an aging mixture (moss and buttermilk) as soon as the casting is removed from the mold. The moss will start to grow as the planter cures. See "Creating a Mossy Finish" in the Cement Casting section.

10. Let Cure

Leave the planter to cure for 2 to 3 weeks.

Photo 1 – Filling the mold. A trowel is used to add the casting mix to the space between the bowls. The tamping stick is nearby. The hypertufa was mixed in a plastic tub.

Photo 2 – Removing the mold.

Hypertufa Trough

Once you have made a smaller planter, try a larger trough-style planter. I used plastic bins for my molds, but you can also use cardboard boxes lined with thin plastic sheeting. You will need to shore up the sides of the boxes with bricks or lumber to prevent them from bowing out and collapsing with the weight of the hypertufa mix. If you plan to make a large container, it is best to cast it where it will eventually end up, saving you from having to move the heavy finished piece.

For the mold, you'll need two plastic containers, one larger and one smaller overall by at least 1-1/2" to 2". Because this is a larger container, the wall should be thicker than those of a smaller round planter.

Use four plastic drainage tubes, spacing them evenly. To make the planter, follow the instructions for "Hypertufa Casting, Step by Step" at the beginning of this section.

Fossil Fern Birdbath

Here a leaf was used as a mold for creating the bowl of this birdbath. The bowl of this cast birdbath sits on a log. The bowl was cast using a sand mound for shape, with leaves to make an impressed pattern. Choose plant material with strong veins, such as sturdy fern fronds or magnolia leaves, and use several leaves to make a pattern.
Ideally, birdbaths should be no more than 2" to 3" deep and have a texture the birds' feet can grasp. The rough surface and gradual slope of this hypertufa birdbath are bird-friendly.
I used a baby wading pool to hold the sand for the mold.

supplies

Hypertufa ingredients (See the list of Basic Supplies at the beginning of this section.)

Large container with sand to make a sand mold

4 to 5 fresh fern fronds

Stick with 1" and 2" markings, to check the depth

Log, 4" diameter, 20" to 24" high, to use as a base

Equipment from list of Basic Supplies at the beginning of this section.

Optional: Outdoor acrylic paints for decorating, wire mesh strips for a sturdier casting, two-part epoxy coating to make the birdbath watertight

instructions

1. Construct a sand mold by dampening the sand and building a shallow mound in the container. Pack down well. Place the leaves on the sand, backside up.
2. Mix the hypertufa casting mix, following the instructions for "Hypertufa Casting, Step by Step."
3. Place handfuls of the mix on top of the fern fronds on the sand mound and form into your desired shape. (See photo 1)
4. Use the marked stick to check the depth of the hypertufa layer. It should be 2" thick in the center and taper to 1" thick at the sides. *Option:* Place one layer of hypertufa mix on the mold. Place wire mesh strips over the first layer. Cover with more mix.
5. Hollow out a depression in the middle of the molded shape 1/2" larger than the diameter of the base (the log). This is to make sure your birdbath sits securely on its base, safe from being tipped over by children or pets. TIP: Have someone place the base over the mix and mark the size, using a stick to make an impression.
6. Place a plastic sheet over the form. Let set for 48 hours.

7. Lift carefully off the sand mound.
8. Call over the hardened shape and leave to cure completely. When cured, brush away the sand and dried fern fronds, leaving the impressions in the sand.
9. *Option:* Paint the fern impressions with outdoor paint. Let dry.
10. *Option:* Cured hypertufa holds water very well, but over time it will weather and may start to leak. To prevent this, after the birdbath fully cured, apply an epoxy coating to the inside to make it waterproof. ❏

Photo 1 – Fossil leaf technique – showing placing the casting mixture on a leaf.

Fossil Leaf Fountain

Large banana palm leaves are used to create this remarkable garden fountain.
Other large leaves that could be used include rhubarb or hosta, among others.
I used a baby wading pool to hold the sand for the mold.

supplies

Hypertufa ingredients (See the list of Basic Supplies at the beginning of this section.)

Large container with sand to make a sand mold

Large leaves

Stick with 1" and 2" markings, to check the depth

Fountain motor and plastic tubing

Thick plastic sheeting, for a pond

Rocks, for the fountain foundation

plus Equipment from list of Basic Supplies at the beginning of this section.

Optional: Outdoor acrylic paints for decorating, wire mesh strips for a sturdier casting, two-part epoxy coating to make the birdbath watertight

instructions

Make the Leaves:

Repeat the process for each leaf. I made two castings for this fountain.

1. Construct a sand mold by dampening the sand and building a shallow mound in the container. Pack down well. Place the leaves on the sand, backside up.
2. Mix the hypertufa casting mix, following the instructions for "Hypertufa Casting, Step by Step."
3. Place handfuls of the mix on top of the leaves on the sand mound and form into a leaf shape. (Photo 1) Use the stick to check the depth of the hypertufa layer. It should be 2" thick in the center tapering to a 1" thickness at the sides. *Option:* Place one layer of hypertufa mix on the leaf. Place wire mesh strips over the first layer. Cover with more mix.
4. Place a plastic sheet over the form and let set for 48 hours before carefully lifting off the sand mound.
5. Turn over the hardened shape and leave to cure. When cured, brush away the excess sand and dried leaves, leaving the leaf impression in the sand.

Construct the Fountain:

I used rocks as a foundation for the fountain, stacking them and positioning the cast leaves. TIP: Arrange the rocks and leaves. When you are satisfied with the arrangement, take it apart and re-stack with the fountain components.

1. Create the fountain by digging a shallow pond to collect and recycle the water. Line it with thick plastic. Install the fountain motor.
2. Rim the pond with rocks to make a reservoir.
3. Stack the rocks and hypertufa leaves so they form a waterfall into the pond, placing the tubing for the water to flow to the top. ❏

Metric Conversion Chart

Inches to Millimeters and Centimeters

Inches	MM	CM	Inches	MM	CM
1/8	3	.3	2	51	5.1
1/4	6	.6	3	76	7.6
3/8	10	1.0	4	102	10.2
1/2	13	1.3	5	127	12.7
5/8	16	1.6	6	152	15.2
3/4	19	1.9	7	178	17.8
7/8	22	2.2	8	203	20.3
1	25	2.5	9	229	22.9
1-1/4	32	3.2	10	254	25.4
1-1/2	38	3.8	11	279	27.9
1-3/4	44	4.4	12	305	30.5

Yards to Meters

Yards	Meters	Yards	Meters
1/8	.11	3	2.74
1/4	.23	4	3.66
3/8	.34	5	4.57
1/2	.46	6	5.49
5/8	.57	7	6.40
3/4	.69	8	7.32
7/8	.80	9	8.23
1	.91	10	9.14
2	1.83		

Index